Essential
England

by

ADAM HOPKINS and GABRIELLE MACPHEDRAN

Adam Hopkins is a travel writer and a regular contributor
to the London *Daily Telegraph*. He and Gabrielle
MacPhedran, a journalist and broadcaster, have written
several *Essential* guides.

Little, Brown and Company
Boston   Toronto   London

FIRST U.S. EDITION

The contents of this publication are believed correct at the time of printing.
Nevertheless, the publishers cannot accept responsibility for errors or
omissions, nor for changes in details given. We are always grateful to readers
who let us know of any errors or omissions they come across, and future
printings will be updated accordingly.

Produced by the Publishing Division of The Automobile Association of Great
Britain.

Written by Adam Hopkins and Gabrielle MacPhedran
''Peace and Quiet'' section by Paul Sterry
Series Adviser: Ingrid Morgan
Series Controller: Nia Williams

ISBN 0-316-25019-8

10 9 8 7 6 5 4 3 2 1

PRINTED IN TRENTO, ITALY

INTRODUCTION 4

BACKGROUND 6

LONDON 16

EAST ANGLIA, THE FENS
AND LINCOLN 36

MIDDLE ENGLAND 48

THE NORTH 64

THE SOUTH 80

THE SOUTHWEST 91

PEACE AND QUIET
  Wildlife and Countryside
  in England 105

FOOD AND DRINK 114

SHOPPING 114

ACCOMMODATION 116

CULTURE, ENTERTAINMENT
AND NIGHTLIFE 116

WEATHER AND
WHEN TO GO 117

HOW TO BE A LOCAL 117

CHILDREN 118

TIGHT BUDGET 119

SPECIAL EVENTS 119

SPORTS 120

DIRECTORY 121

INDEX 127

This book employs a
simple rating system to
help choose which
places to visit:

◆◆◆   do not miss

◆◆   see if you can

◆   worth seeing if
      you have time

INTRODUCTION

The whole of this book is an attempt to answer the question: why England? And the answer must take as many shapes and forms as the cities, towns and villages, landscapes, abbeys, churches and cathedrals, country houses, palaces and museums with which the country is so liberally endowed. England is just one part of a United Kingdom which also includes Wales, Scotland and Northern Ireland (and never confuse the parts with the whole); it is astonishingly rich in places which are worth a visit.

By the same token, England can offer plenty in terms of kings and queens, of ancient bishoprics, of dukes and earls, of knights and ladies. It all adds up to a rather cosy kind of heritage, but one which some natives embrace with enthusiasm. They may not be so proud of the imperial phase which followed. But nobody can deny that it was in these islands that there originated a language now used across the world. Chaucer, Shakespeare, Milton, Keats and Byron: great poets made the English language, along with traders, farmers, sailors, adventurers, husbands, wives, daughters and sons.

Another aspect is the greenness of the countryside, even in midsummer. Though considerable areas were transformed into cityscape by the Industrial Revolution of the 18th and 19th centuries, and further areas have gone down under concrete in the 20th, a large part of England remains unspoiled at first glance. Sometimes the country towns seem to be living out a kind of rural idyll in a setting that must still bear a close resemblance to the 'green and pleasant land' so praised by the poet William Blake 200 years ago. As for 'the dark satanic mills' of industry, whose impact Blake also recorded, it is undoubtedly true that urban dreariness persists in parts. But many cities have begun to repair and remake themselves for a post-industrial age. There is a strong sense that urban Britain is once more on the move, revealing some of the most fascinating elements of her industrial heritage.

English gardens are among the finest in Europe. Stourhead, Wiltshire (west of Stonehenge) is an 18th-century Italianate extravaganza

England may be small but it is concentrated. Regional differences remain strong – not so much in food, perhaps, though they exist, but certainly in attitude, mirrored in voice and accent. Even in bordering regions like Cornwall and its neighbour Devon, the differences, and the sense of difference, are strong. There are national borders in Europe which mean a good deal less than the crossing over the River Tamar from Devon into Cornwall.

All this being said, one major attraction is still awaiting mention. This is London, capital city with a world ranking, unfolding itself for the visitor not just as an historic site but as a city that is enormously alive. London above all requires thorough sampling.

Visitors will almost inevitably approach through the historic England, and that is certainly a valid way to start. But in the end, what matters most must be the contact individuals make with the English present. Here, perhaps, London is the natural starting point. But out beyond it lies the whole of a 20th-century country that is just as rich in interest as any image conjured from the past.

BACKGROUND

What we call Britain began as part of Europe.
It was the flood waters at the end of the Ice
Age which made it into an island, separated
from the continental land-mass by a stretch of
water that the English call the Channel. But
the sea was more a highway than a barrier
and, from the beginning, invasions from the
mainland came in never-ceasing waves. By
3000BC the island's residents were building
on a mighty scale – huge mounds and
standing stones and burial chambers large
and grand enough to astonish. The Celts
arrived, bringing with them a sense of
mystery and magic which still exists in the
parts of Britain where they live on today – in
Wales, particularly, but also in England,
above all in Cornwall, in the far west.

The Romans
Julius Caesar invaded the island in 55BC and
again the following year. But Roman
settlement only began after the invasion by
the Emperor Claudius in AD43. The natives

put up a hopeless fight. One early resistance heroine was Boadicea, or Boudicca, Queen of the Iceni. A statue showing her in her chariot, hair flying in the wind, stands at the end of Westminster Bridge, opposite the Houses of Parliament.

The Romans brought all the advantages of a highly developed civilisation. They built a network of roads, towns, villas, palaces, baths and garrisons. They brought trade and learning and new farming methods. Towns like Colchester, St Albans, York and London thrived and prospered. They settled mostly in England and kept out the unruly Scots by the simple method of building a wall, named after the Emperor Hadrian, across the northern limits of the country.

When the great Roman empire began to fall apart, they withdrew from Britain leaving it a prey to successive waves of invasion by northern European tribes. The Saxons, Angles and Jutes all came and conquered. Even the legendary heroes, King Arthur and his knights, could not withstand them.

Anglo-Saxons vs Vikings

When St Augustine arrived in Kent on his evangelising mission in 597, the Anglo-Saxons converted to Christianity in droves and Canterbury became the seat of the archbishop. The English church was soon renowned for its learning.

The invasions continued. This time the Vikings – Norwegians and Danes – took the Orkney and Shetland islands, moved down to East Anglia and Mercia (the central part of England) and up into Northumbria. The areas of the country under their control became known as the Danelaw. The Saxons resisted and, for a period, there was a see-sawing balance of power between them. After the death of Viking king Cnut, the succession was up for grabs again. Eventually, William of Normandy – one of the group of Norsemen who had settled in France – not only advanced his claim but won it by force of arms against the Saxon claimant, Harold. In 1066 at the battle of Hastings, the last successful invasion of England took place.

BACKGROUND

Normans Ascendant

The Norman presence is strong in England –
churches, cathedrals and castles abound as
proof that William's conquest was successful
and long term. While he was king of England,
though, he was also king of his territories in
France. This double role was an important
feature of English medieval kingship and
proved extremely problematic. By the time
King John (1199–1216) came to the throne, the
growing poverty of the crown and his reliance
on the financial support of his barons in
fighting for his French possessions forced him
to cave in to their demands. This had far
reaching effects. The document he signed at
Runnymede in 1215 was Magna Carta, the
Great Charter. Essentially, it put a limit to his
own authority in relation to the barons. At the
time it was little more than the victory of a
small but powerful faction. Today it is seen as
a significant step towards representative
government.

The French possessions slowly fell away, and
a great deal of wealth and life was lost in the
bitter wars between their French and British
claimants. The English throne itself was the
subject of a tug-of-war between the House of
York, whose symbol was a white rose, and
the House of Lancaster, symbolised by a red
rose. The Wars of the Roses were only
resolved when Henry VII, from the Welsh
Tudor and Lancastrian lines, married
Elizabeth of York in 1485 and began the
Tudor dynasty.

Tudor Renaissance

The Tudor period, beginning with Henry VII
in 1485 and ending with the death of Queen
Elizabeth I in 1603, is synonymous in most
people's minds with a kind of renaissance,
reaching its peak under Elizabeth. The
country was relatively peaceful and had
grown wealthy from increased trade. The
Spanish Empire was on the wane; in 1577
Francis Drake circumnavigated the world
and in 1588 England defeated the Spanish
Armada. This was the England of the poet
Edmund Spenser, the scientist-philosopher
Francis Bacon, the dramatists Christoper

Marlowe and William Shakespeare.
Henry VIII (1509–47) is famous for his six
wives. His much married state was less a sign
of amorousness than an expression of the
need for a male heir. The breach with the
Church of Rome, brought on by his divorce,
combined with a host of other factors to
launch the English Reformation. It led to a
separate Church of England and ever-
widening strife between Protestantism and
Catholicism.

Stuarts on the Throne

Elizabeth I was succeeded by the Stuart
James VI of Scotland, now James I of England.
By the time his son, Charles I (1625–49), came
to the throne, Catholicism had come to be
associated with unchecked royal power and
archaic ways (the Cavaliers); non-conformism
with robust new thinking and a leaning
towards democratic government
(Roundheads). The latter won but only
through a bitterly fought civil war, culminating
in the execution of the king. After a king-less
period under Oliver Cromwell, the Stuarts
were brought back, with Charles II, son of the
executed monarch, succeeding to the throne.
This was the Restoration, a brilliant period in
science and the arts.

It came to an end as the direct result of James
II's strong inclination towards Catholicism.
Now it was his Dutch son-in-law, William of
Orange, who emerged at the head of the

*The British Civil
War is not forgotten:
societies all over
England still fight it
out – without
bloodshed*

Protestant cause, landing in England in 1688 to stage the Bloodless Revolution. Never again would England be Catholic. The price that William and his wife Mary paid for the throne was a pact with the nobility which meant effective power-sharing between the monarch and his greater subjects. Out of this, there evolved a modern parliamentary system based on representation.

Georgians: Age of Elegance

With Anne Stuart's death in 1714, the succession fell to George of Hanover. George was a German prince who spoke no English but he was eminently well qualified in one respect – he was a Protestant. At a period when elegance was asserting itself in art and architecture, political 'parties' were also emerging. The king came to rely on a group of advisers or ministers, particularly on his Prime Minister.

Britain's overseas possessions were now growing at an enormous rate. The spoils of the Seven Years War alone (1756-63) included Canada and India. The American Colonies, founded in the 17th century, were lost in 1783 after their long war of independence.

Victoria Imperatrix

No monarch was more aptly named than this small, stout personage who greatly enlarged the empire she had inherited and at home presided over social changes more drastic than any which had ever before happened in Britain. Steam engines, power looms, roads, canals and railways were making Britain the workshop of the world. Workshops, though, were often sweatshops and conditions were shockingly inhuman. Meanwhile, Karl Marx worked on his Communist Manifesto (published in 1848) in the reading room of the British Library, convinced that when the revolution began, it would be in the industrialising countries. The work of

Queen Victoria watches modern England with a waxen eye

Victorian philanthropists in changing the laws to improve the conditions of working life, the existence of an empire to escape to, plus the slow liberalisation of voting laws, defused the bomb that Marx had glimpsed. This was the age of Dickens.

Twentieth Century

Two world wars have changed England's
certainties and social hierarchy – though
visitors are still astonished by the extent to
which social class persists. The Empire has
gone, swiftly and sometimes painfully.
Meanwhile, England has become culturally
and ethnically far more diverse, with the
arrival of many Caribbean and Asian families.
An economic upswing in the '50s was
followed in the '60s and '70s by a period of
decline, itself accompanied by industrial
unrest. It was also a period of extraordinary
cultural ebullience, most spectacular among
the young but reaching almost everyone. The
Beatles established England as a world
centre of rock music while young people
donned ever more colourful garb, making
London a dream city for the visiting
photographer.
The '80s, Mrs. Thatcher's decade, were
greeted by some visitors as an era of hope for
a new Britain – streamlined, competitive,
willing to embrace change. Others saw the
country as harsher, more ruthless and more
divided. Following Thatcher's departure, a
more balanced estimate will in due course be
possible. At all events, Britain is now a
member of the European Community and
moving fast into a post-industrial age. It is an
exciting time to live in England, an exciting
time to visit.

English Architecture

As seems to be universally the case, the
greatest monuments in England are religious
and military. One may see their start in the
Stone Age megaliths and huge earthworks of
the Iron Age hill-forts. The Romans, as
Hadrian's Wall and the temples along its
length attest, were specialists in both the
military and religious fields. The few
surviving Saxon churches are naïve in
comparison.
In architecture as in history, it was the
Normans who launched England on its path
towards the medieval and the modern. They
started colossal building programmes, so that
what is known elsewhere as Romanesque

is called Norman in England. Of all the Norman building that survives, perhaps the best example, most perfect and triumphal, is Durham Cathedral in the north of England. Norman castle building was just as earnest as might be expected, based above all on a strong defensive keep. The Tower of London is the prime example. But Norman intentions can be discerned all over the country, even in such distant and tiny spots as Clun, on the English side of the Welsh border, where ruins rise from a meadow above the little river.

In churches and cathedrals, the next step was the arrival of the pointed arch, not just a neat solution to pressing problems of construction but perpetually lovely to the human eye.

On the Continent, the arrival of the pointed arch and its relations marks the start of the Gothic style. In England, the term 'Gothic' has generally yielded to three sub-divisions: Early English (1150–1290), Decorated (1290–1350) and Perpendicular (1350–1550). These customary divisions are linked to the erection of key buildings, but in practice, most cathedrals and some churches took so long to build that several styles were followed in succession, with builders proudly keeping up to date. Hereford Cathedral, for example, has portions in each and every one of the three styles and even parts that are transitional between Early English and Decorated.

Early English, as might be expected, is relatively simple. Tracery often consists merely of a quatrefoil (or four-leafed) opening pierced in the space left above paired windows. With Decorated, surface decoration on stone proliferates and the beautiful S-curve of the ogee arch is introduced (Wells Cathedral, begun in 1290, is the supreme example). Perpendicular concentrates on height, while window tracery, dedicated mainly to the vertical, is accordingly more austere. But ribbing blossoms out of the high columns to form the exquisite shapes of fan-vaulting. The chapel of King's College, Cambridge, founded by Henry VI in 1441, is one of the loveliest examples.

While Gothic was developing, castle-building

Perpendicular fan-vaulting at its soaring best in King's College Chapel, Cambridge

also took a new turn. Emphasis on the keep gave way to systems in which the whole perimeter was built to be defensible. The results were often immense – witness the great fortifications put up by Edward I in the 13th century to hold down Wales. This tendency reached its final, most complete form in Berwick-upon-Tweed, when defences ordered up against the Scots by Queen Elizabeth turned the whole town into a modern fortress, with bastions and ramparts, allowing the external walls to be protected by its own cannons.

From now on, until the great population expansion of the 19th century, England was well enough equipped with churches and far fewer were built. The exception came with emergencies like the Great Fire of London, when Sir Christopher Wren (1632–1723), generally regarded as the greatest architect in British history, was called in to replace the old St Paul's, burned in the fire, with a magnificient classical structure. He also designed some 50 new churches for the City of London. Come the mid-19th century, though, it was back to Gothic style for the many additional churches now required, with the architect Pugin in the lead, and the Gothic-revival philosophy of John Ruskin dominant. This was a period of great architectural riches, now increasingly appreciated.

BACKGROUND

An honoured guest: Queen Elizabeth I visited Melford Hall in Long Melford, Suffolk in 1578 and is now immortalised in stained glass

Grand Style and Country Houses

The first great houses of the aristocracy, unsurprisingly, were domesticated castles. As peace became more certain, so the unfortified country house developed, becoming one of the great glories of England. Some of the earliest were Tudor and Jacobean, in glossy black and white with timbering revealed. Under the Stuarts, and spectacularly so in the case of Inigo Jones, classicism, based on the work of Palladio, arrived. The best and purest example is the Queen's House at Greenwich, finished in 1635. Wren was also active in domestic architecture, borrowing from Holland the harmonious ensemble of brick and stone, with wide-spreading cornice and front door under a wide pediment, that we now think of as entirely English. This led on one hand to the dashing and marginally medieval classicism of his pupil Hawksmoor, more than matched by that of his contemporary Vanbrugh, and on the other to the neatly beautiful proportions of the Queen Anne house.

Some of the houses of the late 17th and early 18th centuries, like Chatsworth in Derbyshire or Blenheim in Oxfordshire, were to all intents and purposes private palaces. Others were more domestic in scale, in a tradition which has continued right up to the present day. No account can end, indeed can even be said to have made a beginning, without mention of three great 18th-century names: William Kent, not only architect but artist and gardener; Robert Adam, designer of exquisite interiors; and Lancelot 'Capability' Brown, unafraid of the attempt to improve on nature and leading proponent of the characteristic English 'park' around great houses.

Most of the older examples are now open to the public, and whether one's interest is in the greatest or the not-so-great, visiting them can be among the most rewarding aspects of a tour of England.

Gardens

The English have always been gardeners and there are many hundreds of gardens open to the public, with a majority, naturally enough, in the south and southwest. They range from back gardens of council houses (state-assisted public housing, that is to say) to the very grandest establishments. Naturally, the gardens of the great houses followed evolving style, from the intricacy of the Elizabethan knot garden, through the formality of baroque and on to a handsome floral rebirth in the Victorian era. Some believe the greatest flourish of all was in the Edwardian era, earlier in the present century, with such gifted informal gardeners as Gertrude Jekyll. For those with an interest, gardens must rank with parish churches, castles and country houses as a virtually inexhaustible touring theme.

The People's Architecture

The domestic architecture of England is endlessly fascinating. Despite appearances (and what you might be led to believe), medieval survivals are few. The fact is that medieval forms persisted well beyond the period defined by more formal architecture, helping to give English villages and towns a timeless look. With black-and-white Tudor and Jacobean, above all along the Welsh border and through Shakespeare country, you are on surer ground, at least in terms of the origin of a style which has been much imitated later.

One of the greatest joys is the use of local building materials – the honeyed stone of the Cotswolds, the flint walls and hung tiles of the South, the sterner stone of the Derby Peak District, the red brick and decorative blue 'engineering' brick of the Midlands. Yet another notable English feature is the terrace, long rows of houses joined together on both sides. In Georgian England, above all in Bath, the terrace could be an architectural glory. Often, as in the housing built by the Victorians for the industrial labour force, the saving on outside walls was simply a cheap and space-saving way of building. But even these houses, monotonous though their rows appear to anyone travelling through the backs of towns by railway, are now appreciated for their solidity and flexibility.

LONDON

The reasons for visiting London are almost innumerable. Some people are drawn by royal pageantry. Almost all will wish to begin by knocking off the major sights, from the Houses of Parliament and Westminster Abbey to Piccadilly Circus and Trafalgar Square, and not forgetting the Tower of London, while the museums hold collections as important as any in the world.

For some, London's 'theatreland' is a major draw. Music abounds – whether pop, rock, or classical. Opera and ballet flourish. London's cultural life is matched as an attraction by London's shopping, ranging from the huge department stores of Oxford Street to one-of-a-kind boutiques catering to every taste and need. From the court tailors and fashion houses of the 18th century, on through the era of hard collars and bowler hats to the 'swinging London' of the '60s, to the punks with their bondage gear and bleached Mohawks, and into the present day where anything at all appears to do, London has been at the centre of style.

Then there are the parks. Despite the reputation of the English weather, the London summer can sometimes be halcyon, encouraging visitors to take full advantage of the city's parks and gardens, some 1,700 of them, starting in the very centre and radiating out in every direction.

Equally, visitors can see first class sports, with Wimbledon as one of the world's leading tennis centres, Wembley for soccer, Twickenham for the bizarre sport of rugby football and Lords, the home and hearth of cricket, that even more bizarre British invention. Londoners come in every form imaginable, from the Cockneys of the East End to the host of immigrant communities who have arrived over the centuries, from other parts of Britain, from Ireland, Europe, Asia and Africa. They help to give a distinctive character to different parts of town.

For another of London's characteristics is its 'village' atmosphere, a higgledy-piggledy procession from one area to another, each varying from its neighbour.

Most of the sights and action are concentrated on the northern bank of the river. On the eastern side lie the traditionally less wealthy districts. Back towards the centre, the East End gives way abruptly to the City, London's financial centre. Further westwards, though still very central, lie the West End, the city's entertainment centre, and Westminster, traditional centre of power. Residential districts out to the western flank of the city are richer and more comfortable than those to the east. North and south, the London suburbs stretch endlessly away.

Given the vast size of the city, there is much comfort in the fact that the centre itself is small enough to be easily walkable for most.

London's History

It was the Romans who first settled London, soon after the Emperor Claudius's invasion in AD43. They pulled up their trading ships on the gravel beds of the Thames at the lowest point where they could bridge the river, establishing London Bridge, right from the start, as one of the most vital elements in England's communications. Boadicea burnt the settlement in her revolt of AD61; the Romans responded by throwing up a three-mile (5km) wall right round it. Within this space a major city soon began to grow. William the Conqueror quickly realised London's strategic importance and began to build the Tower of London, one of a chain of castles intended to establish military control across the country.

Later monarchs made their home a few miles upstream among the rural simplicities of Westminster, but by the 17th century, Parliament had set up shop here.

The original City of London had remained independent of Westminster and under the auspices of its Lord Mayor and medieval trade guilds, it grew to be far and away England's biggest city, its most important centre of trade and manufacture.

The land on the south of the river was dismal swamp, a fact which long delayed its settlement. The south bank was to become what it remains – a centre for the entertainment of Londoners. Where once there was bear-baiting, now there is a concert hall. A National Theatre has replaced the round playhouses where Shakespeare's comedies and tragedies were staged.

London became a magnet for settlers from all over the country. They inhabited the crowded, filthy and unhealthy alleyways with timber houses. Tight-packed and busy with its profit-making, the city clustered under the spire of the great Gothic cathedral of St Paul's.

Then, on 2 September 1666, a fire began in a baker's oven on Pudding Lane, a step from the river. The flames roared for

London's burning! The fire of 1666

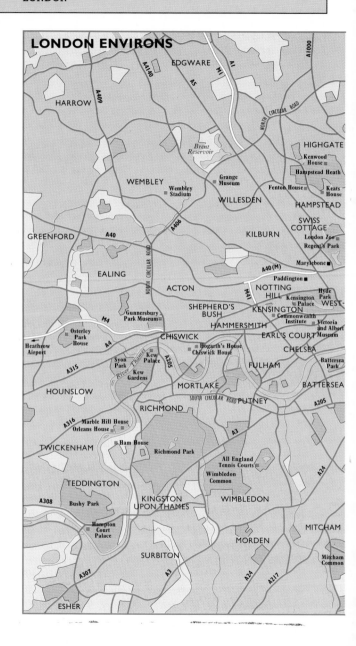

LONDON ENVIRONS

EDGWARE

HARROW

A4140

A409

A5

M1

A1

A1000

NORTH CIRCULAR ROAD

HIGHGATE

Brent
Reservoir

Kenwood
House

Hampstead Heath

WEMBLEY

Wembley
Stadium

Grange
Museum

Fenton House

Keats
House

WILLESDEN

HAMPSTEAD

SWISS
COTTAGE

GREENFORD

A40

A406

KILBURN

London Zoo
Regent's Park

NORTH CIRCULAR ROAD

Marylebone

A40 (M)

EALING

ACTON

Paddington

NOTTING
HILL

Kensington
Palace

Hyde
Park

WEST-

M41

SHEPHERD'S
BUSH

KENSINGTON

Commonwealth
Institute

Victoria
and Albert
Museum

Gunnersbury
Park Museum

HAMMERSMITH

M4

Osterley
Park
House

A4

CHISWICK

EARL'S COURT

Heathrow
Airport

Syon
Park

Kew
Palace

River Thames

Hogarth's House
Chiswick House

CHELSEA

Battersea
Park

A315

Kew
Gardens

A205

FULHAM

BATTERSEA

HOUNSLOW

MORTLAKE

SOUTH CIRCULAR ROAD

PUTNEY

A205

A316

Marble Hill House
Orleans House

RICHMOND

A3

TWICKENHAM

Ham House

Richmond Park

All England
Tennis Courts

A24

Wimbledon
Common

TEDDINGTON

WIMBLEDON

A308

Bushy Park

KINGSTON
UPON THAMES

MITCHAM

Hampton
Court
Palace

MORDEN

Mitcham
Common

A307

SURBITON

A3

A24

A217

ESHER

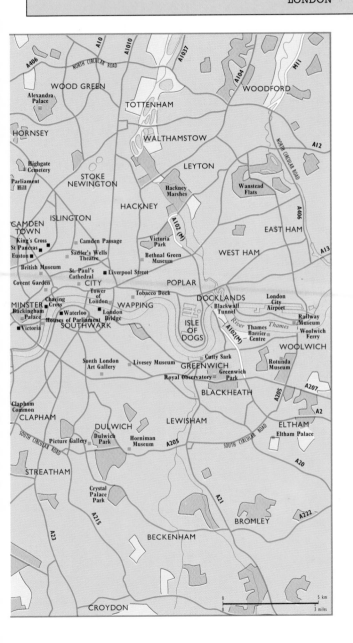

A406
A10
A1010
A1037
A104
M11
NORTH CIRCULAR ROAD
WOOD GREEN
WOODFORD
Alexandra
Palace
TOTTENHAM
HORNSEY
WALTHAMSTOW
NORTH CIRCULAR ROAD
A12
Highgate
Cemetery
LEYTON
Parliament
Hill
STOKE
NEWINGTON
Wanstead
Flats
Hackney
Marshes
A406
HACKNEY
ISLINGTON
CAMDEN
TOWN
EAST HAM
King's Cross
Camden Passage
A102 (M)
Victoria
Park
St Pancras
Euston
Sadler's Wells
Theatre
Bethnal Green
Museum
WEST HAM
A13
British Museum
St. Paul's
Cathedral
Liverpool Street
Covent Garden
CITY
POPLAR
Charing
Cross
Tower
of
London
Tobacco Dock
DOCKLANDS
London
City
Airport
MINSTER
Buckingham
Palace
WAPPING
Blackwall
Tunnel
Railway
Museum
Waterloo
London
Bridge
Houses of Parliament
SOUTHWARK
ISLE
OF
DOGS
A1021(M)
River Thames
Thames
Thames
Barrier
Centre
Woolwich
Ferry
Victoria
WOOLWICH
South London
Art Gallery
Livesey Museum
Cutty Sark
GREENWICH
Rotunda
Museum
Royal Observatory
Greenwich
Park
Clapham
Common
BLACKHEATH
A205
A207
CLAPHAM
LEWISHAM
ELTHAM
A2
DULWICH
Picture Gallery
Dulwich
Park
Horniman
Museum
A205
Eltham Palace
SOUTH CIRCULAR ROAD
SOUTH CIRCULAR ROAD
A20
STREATHAM
Crystal
Palace
Park
A21
A23
A215
BROMLEY
A222
BECKENHAM
0   5 km
3 miles
CROYDON

three days, destroying four-fifths of the city. King Charles II commissioned Sir Christopher Wren, to rebuild the capital.

The city soon resumed its growth. At the end of the 17th century and the start of the 18th it witnessed the foundation of many of its major institutions – Lloyds for insurance, the Stock Exchange and the Bank of England for finances, the Royal Academy for art. Many fine classical façades originated during the 18th century along with the serenity and poise of Georgian domestic architecture.

By the start of the 19th century London had almost a million citizens. Developers now began to fill in whole areas such as Belgravia, giving isolated parts a genuine consistency of style. John Nash, in London's only real attempt at monumental town planning, created the sweeping terraces of Regent's Park and Regent Street. During the rest of the 19th century London burst out of its clothing, sprawling across the countryside. Grand railway stations were erected; along the railway lines the suburbs followed.

Growth has continued right up to the present day, despite the battering London took during World War II, and despite attempts to contain it within a Green Belt (no-building zone). The city which one visits now is Georgian and above all Victorian, with magnificent survivals and some later infilling. There is no end to the discoveries that can be made.

THE CITY

The city of London, or the Square Mile as it is sometimes known, is the oldest part of London, the kernel around which all else has grown. In places the ancient lay-out still exists but the winding lanes and alleyways are overshadowed nowadays by lofty towers housing what has become exclusively a financial centre, Britain's version of Wall Street, complete with Stock Exchange, the ancient insurance exchange of Lloyds (look out for Lloyds' striking 1986 tubular steel building), the Bank of England, affectionately known as the Old Lady of Threadneedle Street, and a host of other financial institutions.

WHAT TO SEE

◆
FLEET STREET
The name of Fleet Street was once synonymous with the British press, but in the last ten years the newspapers have moved away to cheaper sites. Dr Johnson lived just off Fleet Street, in Gough Square. His house survives, containing paintings, memorabilia and the garret where the writer stood to compose his dictionary between 1749 and 1759.

◆
GUILDHALL
King Street, Cheapside
The turreted and stone-tiled Guildhall (1411–40) looks like a secular cathedral with its stained glass windows and vaulted roof. Each year the

Lord Mayor holds a banquet in the Guildhall which is addressed by the prime minister of the day in something close to a state of the union speech. The Lord Mayor also lends his name to London's finest and most traditional procession.

◆
LEGAL LONDON
On the opposite side of the City from Tower Bridge, but still within its western limits, there lies the legal district. In the Gothic revival **Royal Courts of Justice** in the Strand, or the **Old Bailey** close to St Paul's, visitors can see the law in action. The lawyers work in 'chambers' occupying a series of college-like Inns of Court dotted all round this part of the City. **Gray's Inn**, **Lincoln's Inn**, and the **Middle** and **Inner Temples**, their squares and courtyards lined by simple terraces and grander halls, are havens of quiet and some of the most remarkable groups of buildings in the city.

◆
MONUMENT
Monument Street
This tall column was built by Wren near Pudding Lane, the spot where the Great Fire began. There is no elevator, but the energetic may climb it.

◆
MUSEUM OF LONDON
London Wall
The museum successfully recreates the events and everyday life of the capital from Roman times to the Blitz in galleries laid out

chronologically. The museum is effectively linked to the **Barbican Arts Centre**, with theatre, concert hall and galleries.

◆◆◆
ST PAUL'S CATHEDRAL
Ludgate Hill
Built by Sir Christopher Wren on the site of the old St Paul's, this is England's only baroque cathedral. Its dome is the second largest in the world (after St Peter's in Rome). It was in St Paul's that Lady Diana Spencer was married to Prince Charles in a service seen all round the world on televison.

St Paul's glows in the London sky

LONDON

◆◆
TOWER BRIDGE
The bridge's grey stone towers and upper walkways comprise a museum. Climb up for a bird's-eye view of the castle and to see the Victorian steam engines which raise the two sides of the bridge to allow ships to pass.

◆◆◆
TOWER OF LONDON
Tower Hill
The fortifications known generally as the Tower of London, standing guard over the river, were started when William the Conqueror built the keep, the White Tower (1078–97). Successors added towers, a wide sweep of external wall and an enormous moat.

The Tower: castle, prison, museum

The Crown Jewels are displayed here between state occasions; the Royal Armouries hold enough breastplates, cannons and pikes for several armies. On the walls, prisoners of long ago have scrawled their messages. Among those who met their doom here were Anne Boleyn, Sir Walter Raleigh and, earlier (in 1483), the so-called Little Princes.
The Yeoman Warders of the Tower, the red and blue liveried Beefeaters, still live in the Tower. Even more important, at least in legend, is the presence of the six ravens. Should they depart, the Tower will fall to its enemies.

THE WEST END

The West End, confusingly, is
as close as London comes to
having a centre. It occupies
the space between
Westminster and the City, and
is taken up mainly with
shopping and entertainments.
Visitors often come here first,
merely to absorb the
atmosphere. Nightspots,
restaurants and cinemas
abound as well as the more
traditional theatre.

WHAT TO SEE

◆◆
CHINATOWN
London's is smaller than some
other Chinatowns, particularly
in the US, but it is equally
authentic as an Oriental
transplant. It offers cheap (and
expensive) restaurants, exotic
Oriental supermarkets and a
festival of dancing dragons at
the Chinese New Year.

◆◆
COVENT GARDEN
A step beyond Leicester
Square is Covent Garden, with
17th-century church and piazza
designed by the great Inigo
Jones. For centuries it was a
fruit, flower and vegetable
market. But in 1974 the market
was removed and Covent
Garden was made into a place
of pleasure and relaxation.
Today the arcades hold shops,
cafés, and a succession of
street performers, many with
excellent and unusual acts.
The **London Transport
Museum** on the piazza has a
collection of old buses and
trams.

◆◆
OXFORD STREET
Oxford Street is London's
biggest shopping centre,
normally packed on Saturdays,
in summertime generally and,
above all, at Christmas. The
cheaper shops are mostly in its
eastern part; to the west of the
Regent Street crossing lie the
department stores,
considerably more stately,
notably **Selfridges**.

◆◆
PICCADILLY CIRCUS
Piccadilly Circus is the
symbolic centre, a gathering
point for camera-toters and
back-packers, as well as
London's many homeless. The
world-famous **statue of Eros**,
high above a fountain, is ready
again, after long restoration, to
let loose a love-arrow from his
bow. The Circus is gaudy and
inclining to be tacky. There
are amusement arcades and
small permanent exhibitions
aimed at the teenage market –
the Beatles Exhibition, Rock
Circus and fun and freaks of
the Guinness World of
Records in the **Trocadero**.
Close by is **Leicester Square**
with the Hippodrome
nightclub, cinemas and
benches under the handsome
trees.

◆◆
REGENT STREET
Designed by Nash in the 19th
century, and much rebuilt in
imitation of the original, it holds
airline offices and a few stylish
shops like **Burberry's** and
Dickens and Jones. **Liberty**,
reckoned by some to be the
best shop in London, is tucked

in just behind. **Carnaby Street** is also behind Regent Street. Once its cheap and cheerful, outré fashions seemed to symbolise the swinging '60s. Nowadays it mostly sells meretricious junk.

◆◆
SOHO
Soho is the home of Berwick Street market, film studios (round Wardour Street) and London's liveliest streetlife with fruit and vegetable stallholders calling out their wares, stalls laden with records, cheap cassettes and tee-shirts, sexshops and prostitutes (though fewer and tamer than formerly), eateries of all sorts, fashion shops, and media and advertising firms. Through the lower part of Soho, angling up from Piccadilly Circus, runs Shaftesbury Avenue, where Theatreland overlaps with bookshop territory.

Horseguards display their splendour

WESTMINSTER, WHITEHALL AND TRAFALGAR SQUARE

Since the time of Edward the Confessor, Westminster has been the principal royal residence, first in the form of Westminster Palace (the current parliament), then in a huge sprawl of palace in Whitehall, destroyed by fire in the 17th century, except for its Banqueting House, and currently in Buckingham Palace. The court followed the King and it was natural that Parliament should make its permanent home in Westminster.

WHAT TO SEE

◆◆◆
BUCKINGHAM PALACE AND THE MALL
Crossing **St James's Park**, one of London's prettiest, the visitor will see the grey and uninspiring façade of Buckingham Palace. A standard is flown to signal that the Queen is at home. At the

left side of the palace, on Buckingham Gate, is the **Queen's Gallery** with a small collection of Royal memorabilia. Beyond again are the **Royal Mews** (or stables), designed by Nash and housing the Queen's magnificent coaches.

The **Changing of the Guard** involves a ceremonial march along the Mall with the final hand-over at Buckingham Palace at 11:30A.M. (every other day in winter). Other major royal pageants include the **State Opening of Parliament** in late October and the **Trooping of the Colour** (main ceremony on Horseguards' Parade) on the Queen's official birthday, the second Saturday in June. Also on the Mall is the **Institute of Contemporary Arts** which holds talks, film-shows and exhibitions, mainly avant-garde.

♦♦♦
HOUSES OF PARLIAMENT
St Margaret Street

Big Ben is technically the huge bell that tolls the hours above the Houses of Parliament. Londoners use the name for the clock itself, its face 23 feet (7m) across, high up on the Gothic revival tower that rises above the river. Except for its medieval hall, virtually the whole of the present building (officially still the Palace of Westminster) is a 19th-century construction in medieval style. There are two debating chambers, one for the House of Lords (red leather benches) and one for the House of Commons (green benches).

Big Ben and the Houses of Parliament

Visitors may attend parliamentary debates (held in the afternoon and evening – wait in line at St Stephen's entrance).

♦♦♦
NATIONAL GALLERY
Trafalgar Square

The National Gallery (a classical building of 1838 with a modern extension opened in 1991) houses one of northern Europe's leading international collections, with masterpieces of all periods. Here, for instance, Velázquez's *Rokeby Venus* shares wall-space with Leonardo da Vinci's *Virgin of the Rocks*, while the English contribution includes Constable's *Hay Wain* and Turner's *Rain, Steam and Speed*. This is a gallery not to be missed.

◆
NATIONAL PORTRAIT GALLERY
St Martin's Place
This is a gathering-place for paintings, sculptures and photographs of almost everybody of significance in British history. Arranged chronologically, beginning on the second floor, it gives a strong sense of the changes in English society over the centuries.

◆
ST MARTIN-IN-THE-FIELDS
St Martin's Place
This porticoed church of classical style (1722-4), improbably topped off with a steeple, is a familiar and much-loved part of the London scene.

St Martin-in-the-Fields

◆◆◆
TATE GALLERY
Millbank
The Tate is complementary to the National Gallery and home to notable collections: Turner (more than 300 of his oil-paintings in the recently opened Clore Gallery extension), British painting from 1600 (good collections of Blake and Constable, for instance) and international and British modern art. Quite outstanding – highly recommended.

◆◆◆
TRAFALGAR SQUARE
Here **Nelson's Column**, commemorating his victory at the naval battle of Trafalgar (1805) and with four handsome lions at its base, is the obvious focus. Londoners gather in the square in summer. Visitors feed the dense flocks of pigeons and have their photos taken. Major political demonstrations and rallies often end here. Huge crowds come on New Year's Eve to see the old year out.

◆◆◆
WESTMINSTER ABBEY
Parliament Square
Westminster Abbey is the unofficial church of court and Parliament. Since the coronation of William the Conqueror here, on Christmas Day 1066, all but two of England's monarchs have been crowned before the High Altar.
The present building was erected between the 13th and 16th centuries. Beyond the high, narrow nave, pillars,

Magnificent Westminster Abbey

partitions and the sheer number of memorials break the Abbey up into a series of chapels and private-seeming spaces, grandest of which is the Henry VII Chapel with its Tudor tombs and ornate stalls. In Poets' Corner lie many of England's greatest writers. Handel is also buried in the Abbey. By the west door is the Tomb of the Unknown Soldier. There is so much fascinating detail that it is worth taking the guided tour (one and a half hours).

◆◆
WHITEHALL
Here, behind the impressive façades, among them Gilbert Scott's handsome Foreign Office (1868–73) and the blanker modernity of the Ministry of Defence, is the real machinery of government. On the street of Whitehall itself there are statues of imperial heroes, and the **Cenotaph** commemorating the dead of two world wars. Through the security gates can be seen the doors of **No 10 Downing Street**, home to the Prime Minister, now barred to the public. In Inigo Jones's beautiful **Banqueting House**, last remnant of Whitehall Palace, the ceiling painting of *The Apotheosis of James I* is by Rubens. Charles I was beheaded here in 1649. Just off Whitehall, and on the corner of Horseguards' Parade, are the **Cabinet War Rooms**, the deep bunker from which Churchill conducted World War II, now opened as an atmospheric museum.

KNIGHTSBRIDGE, BOND STREET AND PICCADILLY

West of Piccadilly Circus, fashionable shops and elegant houses, (generally now offices) replace razzmatazz. On the thoroughfare of Piccadilly, the **Ritz Hotel** is perhaps the most famous of London's hostelries. Taking tea at the Ritz means glimpsing a wealthy and handsomely old-fashioned London, akin in some respects to the gentlemen's clubs of St James's and Pall Mall. Some of London's most stylish shopping is here. **Fortnum and Mason**, directly opposite the Royal Academy in Piccadilly, is the country's leading gourmet grocer. **Jermyn Street** behind is a haven of men's shirts, ties and fashion accessories, but also features top parfumiers and London's leading cheese shop. The **Burlington Arcade**, Britain's earliest covered shopping mall, dating from 1819, caters to the top end of the market. So do Bond Street and New Bond Street. **Sotheby's**, the auctioneers, in New Bond Street, and **Christie's** (in King Street on the far side of Piccadilly), offer a chance to see the theatre of the nod and hammer as antiques and paintings go down for terrifying sums. Mayfair, up from Piccadilly at the Hyde Park end, is a tight-packed village for the wealthy, with the US Embassy at its centre in Grosvenor Square. In Knightsbridge, a short distance west, the most famous feature of all is **Harrods** department store.

WHAT TO SEE

◆◆
MUSEUM OF MANKIND
Burlington Gardens
This is the ethnographic section of the British Museum, a brilliant display of the art and everyday objects of distant cultures, ancient and modern. It is one of London's major venues, with a strong appeal for children as well as adults.

◆◆
ROYAL ACADEMY
Burlington House, Piccadilly
The Royal Academy stands in its private courtyard, a grandly classical building, headquarters to Britain's established artists since the days of Sir Joshua Reynolds in the 18th century. Shows range from the Summer Exhibition, selected from previously unseen work by British artists, to key international exhibitions.

Quietly avoiding Speaker's Corner

KENSINGTON AND HYDE PARK

Kensington is mostly a fashionable residential area, with tall stuccoed row houses. Kensington High Street, though, is for shoppers: many successful designers have stalls in **Hyper Hyper** at the top end of the High Street; **Kensington Market** across the road is for the young and trendy.

Many of London's largest and most interesting museums are grouped together in South Kensington. All are easily accessible from South Kensington underground station.

WHAT TO SEE

♦♦
HYDE PARK

In **Speaker's Corner** in the northeast of the park people daily exercise their special right of assembly, addressing small crowds on any issue that

occurs to them. Near by is the triumphal **Marble Arch**. Once, the cream of society rode along **Rotten Row**, a sandy trackway through the park. You can take a boat or swim in the curvaceous lake appropriately named the **Serpentine**. Hyde Park abuts immediately on **Kensington Gardens** and here one may visit the **Serpentine Gallery** (avant-garde artworks) or inspect the gaudy, needle-pointed **Albert Memorial**. Just opposite is the **Albert Hall**, the setting for the 'Proms', a special summer season of cheap concerts.

♦♦
KENSINGTON PALACE

Kensington Palace, at the far end of Kensington Gardens, has been in royal occupation since the time of William and Mary. The state rooms of the comfortable, homelike palace, with formal Dutch gardens and an Orangery, are open to the public. The Court Dress collection ranges from formality to frippery.

♦♦♦
NATURAL HISTORY MUSEUM

Cromwell Road, South
This museum occupies one of Britain's most remarkable 19th-century buildings. From outside it is a Gothic extravaganza in blue and terracotta. Its vaulted and ornately decorated interior is magnificent, with displays featuring all kinds of interactive exhibits. The Life galleries show dinosaur skeletons, a re-created dodo and a simulated womb.

◆◆◆
SCIENCE MUSEUM
Exhibition Road
Exhibits range from milk-churns to offshore oil-drilling gear. They include the steel and traction of the 19th century, modules and rockets of the space age and modern micro-chips.

◆◆◆
VICTORIA AND ALBERT MUSEUM
Cromwell Road/Exhibition Road
This splendid museum of applied and decorative art contains furniture, costumes, ironwork, carpets, china, glass – even whole stairwells and house fronts. Artefacts are from all periods and cultures.

Greek treasures in the British Museum

BLOOMSBURY AND POINTS NORTH

Bloomsbury lies north of Oxford Street and east of Tottenham Court Road (shopping mecca for electronic and photographic goods). It is where you will find the main buildings of London University and, most noble and prestigious of all, the British Museum. This part of London also boasts such tourist honeypots as Madame Tussaud's.

WHAT TO SEE

◆◆◆
BRITISH MUSEUM
Great Russell Street
The museum is monumental in every sense. It holds an enormous collection housed in no fewer than 90 galleries. Roman, Greek, Egyptian, Oriental and Western Asian collections have their local parallel in ancient and medieval British exhibits. There are also manuscripts, prints and drawings. Among the exhibits are the bitterly controversial Elgin Marbles, and the Rosetta Stone, from ancient Egypt, key to the decipherment of hieroglyphics.
The famous library at the core of the museum, with desks radiating like spokes under a high dome, is shortly moving to new accommodation.

◆◆
MADAME TUSSAUD'S
Marylebone Road
This, the single most visited attraction in London, houses

models of the famous and the infamous. Perhaps the big draw is the Chamber of Horrors, with gruesome scenes of torture, murder and mayhem. You may have to wait in line.

The neighbouring **Planetarium** takes visitors on a journey through the night sky (no under 5s) while the **Laserium** produces remarkable laser images of all sorts.

◆
REGENT'S CANAL
Out beyond Regent's Park is Camden Town and its cheerful, young people's market at **Camden Lock** on the Regent's Canal. From Camden Town the canal leads into a whole network of waterways, now redundant but once linking London to the industrial Midlands. There is good exploring here by boat or towpath with pretty vistas under curving bridges of locks, barges and gardens.

◆◆
REGENT'S PARK
Perhaps the most pleasant open space in the whole city, the park lies just to the north of Baker Street and Madame Tussaud's. The park itself, and the gracious curve of terraces on the south side of it, were created by John Nash. Queen Mary Rose Garden in summer has displays of every conceivable variety and colour of rose. Also in summer, Shakespeare plays are performed in the **Open Air Theatre**. **London Zoo**'s future is now uncertain; it may close if state funds are withdrawn.

THE RIVER
For centuries, the Thames has carried the commerce which made London great. Its numerous bridges give fine views, and boat-trips from Embankment or Westminster Piers can give a new perspective on the city, especially on a sunny day.

WHAT TO SEE

◆
DOCKLANDS
Eastwards by boat, or by the new Docklands Light Railway from Tower Hill, lie the Docklands. London was the world's largest port in the 19th century but the docks began to decline after World War I. Since the 1980s a massive regeneration programme has been under way, and a new city-within-a-city is growing up, complete with housing, offices, airport and leisure facilities. **Canary Wharf** on the Isle of Dogs is the most spectacular of the new developments, a glitter of steel and glass, with The Canary Wharf Tower, at 850 feet (260m), far and away England's tallest building. There are vistas across water, where the old dock basins have been moulded into the new development, along the river warehouses have been converted into expensive riverside apartments.

◆◆
GREENWICH
Greenwich encapsulates London's maritime past. Wren harmonised the two wings of his palatial **Royal Hospital** for

sailors (1696–1702) with Inigo Jones's **Queen House** (beautiful interiors, 1616–35) further back from the river. This architectural ensemble is considered by some to be the most perfect in Britain. Other highlights include the **National Maritime Museum**, the *Cutty Sark* (a perfectly preserved tea clipper), the **royal park** with its magnificent views of the Docks and City, and the **Royal Observatory** (straddling the Meridian Line which separates eastern and western hemispheres). Greenwich's village hosts an excellent crafts market every Sunday.

◆◆
HAMPTON COURT
Beyond Kew is Hampton Court, one of the great palaces of the London area. Built originally for Cardinal Wolsey, it was seized by Henry VIII and remained a royal residence for centuries. William and Mary made it their main home with substantial additions built for them by Christopher Wren. The intriguing mixture of Tudor grandeur and classical serenity is complemented by a splendid river setting and magnificent gardens. The yew hedge maze looks rather moth-eaten but still manages to trap its willing victims.

◆◆
KEW GARDENS
An hour and a half's boat-trip west from central London lies Kew, home of the Royal Botanic Gardens. Here, you can see more than 50,000 species of trees and plants from all over the world, originally collected for study and experiment, not merely to give pleasure. The great greenhouses are full of a humid and exotic luxuriance – a great place to visit on a cold London day.

◆
THAMES FLOOD BARRIER
Unity Way
Between the Blackwall Tunnel and the Woolwich Ferry, the enormous pontoons of the Thames Flood Barrier swing into place to protect London from high tides. It is much visited.

Hampton Court – fit for a king

SOUTH OF THE RIVER

Most of London's prime tourist sites are concentrated north of the Thames. However, there are things to see in South London, particularly along the river itself.

WHAT TO SEE

◆
DESIGN MUSEUM
Butler's Wharf
Right on the water in Southwark, the museum was opened in 1989 with the help of many of the corporations whose work it celebrates. It gives a designer's view of everyday objects and allows you, with the help of an interactive video, to design a product of your own.

◆
GLOBE THEATRE SITE
When theatres were banned from the City of London in 1574, they moved across the river to Bankside. Here, the works of the actor-playwright William Shakespeare first gained popularity with the London public. A plaque marks the site of Shakespeare's vanished Globe Theatre. The **International Shakespeare Globe Centre** contains models of Elizabethan and Jacobean theatres and a working replica of a 1616 stage. The recently discovered remains of the **Rose Theatre** are another attraction.

◆◆
IMPERIAL WAR MUSEUM
Lambeth Road, Kennington
This was originally the mental hospital of Bedlam. Now it contains an impressive array of machines of destruction and a fine collection of the work of war artists. Above all it tells the human history of war in the 20th century.

◆◆
SOUTH BANK ARTS CENTRE
Opposite Charing Cross station is the South Bank, London's biggest arts centre. The **Royal Festival Hall**, built for the 1951 Festival of Britain, is surrounded by more recent buildings, often criticised for their bunker-like concrete aspects. It features not just the London Philharmonic Orchestra (its resident orchestra) but many of the world's leading soloists, orchestras and conductors. The **National Film Theatre** runs premières and various seasons of films. The **Museum of the Moving Image** illuminates every aspect of the world of cinema, television and video. Then there is the **Hayward Gallery** and, above all, the **National Theatre**. In its three auditoria, it offers enormous variety and verve. Seeing a play here is an essential part of the London experience.

◆
SOUTHWARK CATHEDRAL
London Bridge
An intimate building, the cathedral contains some fine sculpture and a memorial to the 51 who died when the *Marchioness*, a Thames pleasure boat, sank in 1989. Close by is the **London Dungeon**, a small, rather ghoulish museum not suitable for under 10s.

VILLAGE LONDON

What Londoners think of as their villages are in some instances the genuine villages that once lay in the countryside around the city and were duly absorbed as it grew. In other cases, they are closer to being purpose-built developments. All have a strong and distinctive character. Some, like Bloomsbury and Kensington, have already been mentioned. Others are described below.

◆
BELGRAVIA

Grand 19th-century developments made Belgravia into a very posh village indeed. Its dignified streets and squares are lined with security cameras protecting embassies and lavish private homes.

◆
BRIXTON

Brixton has had a dubious reputation since riots in 1981. Its pre-war music halls have long since closed down, but it has a lively market with a strong Afro-Caribbean flavour and plenty of street life.

◆
CHELSEA

The streets giving off King's Road and Sloane Square contain a variety of pretty mews houses and larger blocks, all with an air of exclusivity and gentle retirement. King's Road stood at the forefront of fashion in the 1960s and again in the '70s. It is still a shopping centre but no longer at the cutting edge of fashion. The **National Army Museum** and Wren's **Royal Hospital** (1681–6), for army veterans, overlook the river. Chelsea villagers take their ease in the **Hospital gardens**, and here, in late May, the Royal Horticultural Society holds the annual **Chelsea Flower Show**.

◆
DULWICH

This south London village has a pretty shopping street with a number of fine 18th-century houses, a park and tree-lined roads. **Dulwich Art Gallery** is extremely well-endowed (much of the best work is by Dutch and Flemish masters) and comfortably small.

◆
HAMPSTEAD

Hampstead's steep hill gives excellent views south over London and there are breezy walks to be enjoyed across Hampstead Heath. The shopping streets in the village centre are lively on weekends. Side streets like Church Row and Flask Walk have gracious 18th-century houses. John Keats (1795-1821) lived here in a delightful little house preserved as a museum. Freud's house, further off, is preserved as he left it, complete with couch. In **Hampstead Garden Suburb**, Edwin Lutyens and colleagues made a village for workers so perfect that only the middle classes can afford to live there.

◆
HIGHGATE

This village, dislocated by

steep hills, woods and busy roads, is chiefly famous for its eerie, sprawling **cemetery** containing the remains of many notables. Most visited of all is the grave of Karl Marx (1883), with an impressive bust.

◆
NOTTING HILL
Grand 19th-century developments covered the slopes of Notting Hill. Today the streets are lively and cosmopolitan. In late August, the Afro-Caribbean community holds Europe's largest street festival, the **Notting Hill Carnival**, in the area around Ladbroke Grove. **Portobello Road** has an excellent market for antiques, junk and vegetables, best on the weekend.

Accommodation
The most expensive hotels are in Piccadilly, Mayfair and Knightsbridge. These include the **Ritz**, Piccadilly (tel:(071) 493 8181) and the **Savoy**, Strand (tel:(071) 836 4343). Smaller hotels, often converted houses, include **Blakes Hotel**, Roland Gardens, South Kensington (tel:(071) 370 6701); **Browns**, which takes up 14 houses in Albemarle and Dover Streets (tel:(071) 493 6020); and the **Chesterfield**, Charles Street, Mayfair (tel:(071) 491 2622). You can pay more reasonable prices at the **Claverley**, Beaufort Gardens (tel:(071) 589 8541); the **Elizabeth Hotel**, Eccleston Square (tel:(071) 828 6812), B&B only; or, further to the north, the **Sandringham**, Holford Road, near Hampstead

Bright colours invite you to take part in Notting Hill Carnival

Heath (tel:(071) 435 1569). The **London Tourist Board**, 26 Grosvenor Gardens (tel:(071) 730 3488) can help with any specific accommodation enquiries.

Restaurants
Generally you will find the most expensive restaurants in the West End. For cheaper options try ethnic restaurants, especially in Soho (Italian and Greek), Notting Hill Gate (West Indian), Charlotte Street (Greek and Indian) and the area around Gerrard Street (Chinese).

EAST ANGLIA, THE FENS AND LINCOLN

Draw a straight line up from London to the North Sea and all the land east of this line consists of Lincolnshire and the large bulge of East Anglia, made up of the counties of Suffolk, Norfolk, Cambridgeshire and Essex. This is an area generally distinguished from the rest of the country by its flatness, its wide skies and water, bearing some resemblance to the flatlands of Holland. Indeed it was a Dutch engineer who carried out the huge land-draining programme in the 17th century, which established the basis of East Anglian agriculture. At springtime, tulips and daffodils in the bulb fields around Spalding make visitors wonder if they have inadvertently crossed the North Sea.

Lincolnshire is green and rolling in the north, descending to flat fen country. In the north of East Anglia, the landscape is of marsh and heathland, long rivers and broad estuaries swept by unfettered winds, and small hamlets settled around grand flint churches.

Even **Norwich** and **Cambridge** cannot be described as large towns and an important ingredient in the charm of this area is the opportunity to be solitary. The **Norfolk Broads** in the height of summer rank as a temporary contradiction of this statement.

Towards the south, the rolling hills and wooded valleys of **Suffolk** give the landscape a

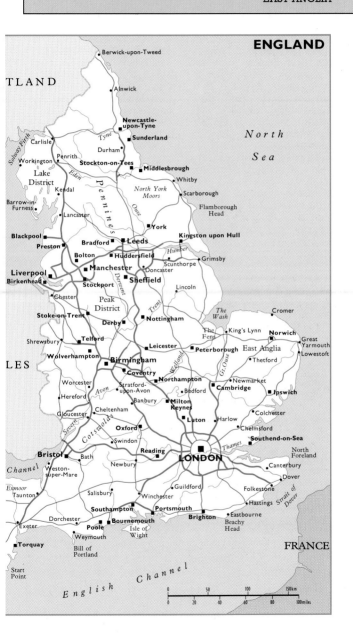

ENGLAND

TLAND

North

Sea

Berwick-upon-Tweed

Alnwick

Newcastle-
upon-Tyne
Tyne
Sunderland
Carlisle
Durham
Solway Firth
Workington
Penrith
Stockton-on-Tees
Lake
District
Middlesbrough
Eden
Whitby
Kendal
North York
Moors
Scarborough
Barrow-in-
Furness
Flamborough
Head
Lancaster
Ouse
York
Blackpool
Kingston upon Hull
Bradford
Leeds
Humber
Preston
P e n n i n e s
Grimsby
Bolton
Huddersfield
Scunthorpe
Liverpool
Manchester
Doncaster
Birkenhead
Stockport
Derwent
Sheffield
Chester
Lincoln
Peak
District
Stoke-on-Trent
Trent
The
Wash
Cromer
Derby
Nottingham
The
Fens
King's Lynn
Norwich
Shrewsbury
Telford
Leicester
East Anglia
Great
Yarmouth
Welland
Peterborough
Lowestoft
Wolverhampton
Thetford
Gt. Ouse
Birmingham
LES
Worcester
Avon
Northampton
Newmarket
Coventry
Stratford-
upon-Avon
Bedford
Cambridge
Ipswich
Hereford
Banbury
Milton
Keynes
Gloucester
Cheltenham
Colchester
Severn
Luton
Harlow
Cotswolds
Oxford
Chelmsford
Swindon
Southend-on-Sea
Bristol
Reading
Thames
Bath
LONDON
North
Foreland
Channel
Weston-
super-Mare
Newbury
Canterbury
Exmoor
Guildford
Dover
Taunton
Salisbury
Winchester
Folkestone
Hastings
Strait of
Dover
Southampton
Portsmouth
Dorchester
Brighton
Eastbourne
Exeter
Poole
Bournemouth
Beachy
Head
Weymouth
Isle of
Wight
Torquay
Bill of
Portland
FRANCE
Start
Point
E n g l i s h *C h a n n e l*

0   50   100   150 km
0   20   40   60   80   100 miles

gentler, more rounded aspect. This is the country of John Constable, England's foremost landscape painter; his vast skies, country lanes and cottages, ancient oaks, water mills and churches have become, for many people, a shorthand for the English countryside.

Historically, this region, isolated for centuries by marsh and fen and poor communications from the rest of the country, has always had close ties with Europe. Recently, increased trade with Europe and the decline of London and Liverpool as ports has meant that the seaways of

this coast have come into their own again. The new technology industries centred around Cambridge and the large agribusiness serving these fertile counties have also helped bring them back into the economic mainstream. Despite all this, the people of these counties continue to pride themselves on their independence and non-conformity. The university of Cambridge championed the English reformation, and religious puritanism found firm roots here. Oliver Cromwell came from these parts, as did many of the Pilgrim Fathers. The transatlantic connection

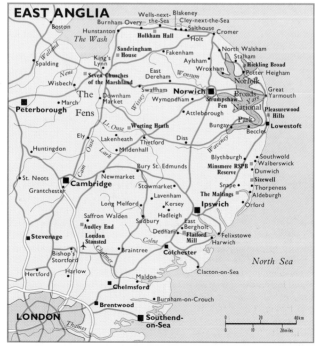

has remained strong ever since. The town of **Boston** in Lincolnshire gave its name to Boston, Massachusetts. In World War II American pilots flew on bombing missions across the North Sea from East Anglian airfields; there are memorials to these men throughout the counties. Even now, the US maintains a number of air bases here. Numerous churches throughout East Anglia have been maintained or renovated by North American generosity. In 1984 the many descendants of the Clopton family returned to England from America to visit their ancestral home, the wool towns of **Hadleigh** and **Long Melford**, and to collect the back rent of 500 years for the ancient Guildhall, leased by their forebear Sir William Clopton. He had demanded, and his heirs received, a single rose for every year.

WHAT TO SEE

◆◆
ALDEBURGH
Suffolk
This small fishing village became a lively focus of cultural life after the composer Benjamin Britten and singer Peter Pears settled here in the 1940s, establishing the annual **Aldeburgh Music Festival**. It has since become the home of musicians, artists and writers. The **Church of St Peter and St Paul**, at the top of the hill overlooking the town, has memorials of former illustrious residents. A stained glass window by John Piper commemorates the life of Benjamin Britten, and there is a bust of the poet George Crabbe, born in Aldeburgh (his poem *The Borough* was the basis of Britten's opera, *Peter Grimes*). In the churchyard, plain dark stones mark the graves of Britten and Pears. Elizabeth Garrett Anderson, the first woman in Britain to qualify as a doctor, is also buried here. Though prevented from practising medicine on grounds of her sex, she was elected the first woman mayor of Aldeburgh (and of England). The house where she lived stands opposite the church.

At **Snape Maltings**, former malthouses and granaries have become the site of many of the events of the Aldeburgh Festival, a few miles inland on the River Alde.

Other villages around Aldeburgh include **Southwold**, where the cannons facing seawards from the village green were a gift from the victorious Duke of Cumberland after the defeat of the Scots in the 1745 Rebellion; and **Dunwich**, where the village is all that remains of the former capital of East Anglia, now mostly under the sea. Locals claim they can hear the bells of their lost churches tolling from beneath the waves when a storm rages.
Thorpeness, also near Aldeburgh, is a curiosity, created in 1910 as a vacation resort by a rich business man, Stuart Ogilvie. The houses are gracious and substantial, set in large floral gardens. Locals

claim that nearby Sizewell nuclear power station warms the waters of the coast.

◆◆
THE BROADS

A well-used but beautiful area of waterways, rivers and lakes in a triangle radiating from Norwich to the coast. The Broads are man-made – **Hickling Broad** is the biggest – and the rivers are shallow; not more than 12 feet (3.5m) deep, even the major ones, the **Bure**, **Yare** and **Waveney**. The towns of **Great Yarmouth**, **Wroxham** and **Potter Heigham** are good centres.

If you are driving through this area, the very flatness of the land can obscure the waterways that are all around you until a sudden glimpse of silvery water, a thin mast behind a hedge or the silent flight of waterfowl past willows, reminds you that you are passing through over 125 miles (200km) of navigable waterways.

Overuse and ignorance, however, have created problems of pollution, with bank erosion, encroaching woodland and loss of wildlife habitat. To counter this, a Broads Authority has been set up with responsibility for conservation and recreation in this area. In the summer, especially, there are accompanied trails, boat trips and rambles with particular emphasis on natural history. For more information contact the **Broads Authority**, 18 Colegate, Norwich NR3 1BQ (tel: (0603) 610734).

◆
BOSTON
Lincolnshire

Once an important sea port and famous as the home of the Pilgrim Fathers, Boston retains close associations with its transatlantic namesake. It also retains the cells in the **Guildhall** into which persecuted Protestants trying to flee to the Low Countries were thrown in 1607. The cells have been restored through American generosity. American money has also restored **St Botolph's** church, where vicar John Cotton, refusing to renounce his Puritan convictions, was forced to quit the living and go to America. For fine views of the area, climb the unfinished tower of the Church, known as **The Boston Stump**.

◆
BURY ST EDMUNDS
Suffolk

More familiarly known as Bury, the town is named after King Edmund, later St Edmund, who was martyred by the Danes in 869. His remains are buried in the **abbey**, now a ruin. Subsequently the town became an important place of pilgrimage. It was here also, in 1214, that determined arm-twisting on the part of some nobles forced King John to accept their political power in the Magna Carta.

The town is an interesting mixture of medieval and Georgian architecture. Watch out for the angel roof and the starred chantry chapel of **St Mary's Church**.

◆◆◆
CAMBRIDGE
Cambridgeshire

With Oxford, this is one of the two most renowned English universities. Its fame is due not only to its academic reputation – Chaucer, Milton and Darwin were all Cambridge graduates, and Erasmus taught here – but to the architectural beauty of its many medieval colleges. The calm and green-banked River Cam and the grounds and gardens that surround the colleges make Cambridge an irresistible destination.

It was founded a little later than Oxford: **Peterhouse**, the oldest college, began its life in 1284. Indeed, it is said to have been an alternative place of learning for some of the more intractable students of the age, and still has a name for rigorous scientific analysis, while Oxford's reputation lies more in the humanities. Many of the older colleges were founded by royal personages and were based on the monastic model – hence the chapels, the communal meals and use of Latin, still part of college life.

Most colleges open their courts or quadrangles, their chapels, and occasionally their refectories and libraries to visitors. But they are primarily residential places for study and at various times some may be closed to the public.

Most of the oldest colleges are concentrated in a small area and situated along the length of one street, known sequentially as **Trumpington Street**, **King's Parade**, **Trinity Street** and **St John's Street**. The **'Backs'** (the backs of the colleges) have college gardens running to the river's edge with open green spaces beyond. The colleges are situated close together and the visitor may stroll through courtyards, buildings and gardens at leisure.

Each college has its own identity and charm but there are a few which are the undisputed stars. **King's College**, founded in 1441 by Henry VI, is one such. The much admired Chapel is built in the Perpendicular style and retains its original stained glass

The Great Gate at Trinity, Cambridge

windows. The fan vaulting is so delicate it looks like fluttering lace. *The Adoration of the Magi* by Rubens stands, simple and magnificent, behind the altar. The choir of King's College Chapel sings at the public service of evensong, held daily in the chapel at 5:30P.M..

Trinity College was founded by Henry VIII and is the wealthiest of the colleges. Its Great Court is also the largest and the traditional sport is to run the circuit around the court while the chapel clock strikes twelve. The library was designed by Christopher Wren, and its bookcases carved by Grinling Gibbons. Former members include Macaulay, Byron, Tennyson and Prince Charles.
William Wordsworth was a member of nearby **St John's**. Here, the famous landmark is the bridge built to emulate the Bridge of Sighs at Venice.
Queens' College is also reached by a bridge: the wooden Mathematical Bridge, so called because it was apparently constructed without nails. Some curious persons dismantled it in the Victorian period but found it impossible to reassemble without the help of nails and screws.
The **Fitzwilliam Museum** in Trumpington Street belongs to the university but offers free access to the public. It houses an outstanding collection of paintings, including work by Turner, Titian and Rembrandt, and Egyptian, Greek and Roman antiquities. **Kettle's Yard Gallery**, at the other end of town, specialises in 20th-century work.
A visit to Cambridge would not be complete without a trip on the river. Punts, canoes or rowboats can be rented from **Scudamoore's** – self- or chauffeur-propelled. Cambridge is best seen on foot. Cars are useless in the already over-busy centre and bicycles, hitherto the traditional mode of transport, have attracted some criticism lately on grounds of numbers and reckless handling. However, they can still be rented by the day.

◆
COLCHESTER
Essex
Colchester is famous in early English history as a hotbed of local resistance against invaders. Cymbeline, the head of the Catavellani tribe, established this town as the Celtic capital and Boadicea, queen of the Iceni, fought the Romans in these parts. The Museum in **Colchester Castle** has excellent Roman exhibits and the Roman town wall is arguably the best preserved in Britain.

◆◆
DEDHAM VALE
Suffolk
East Bergholt in Dedham Vale was the birthplace of the English landscape painter John Constable in 1776, and the subject of many of his paintings. Much of the village is modern, with the oldest parts centred around the pubs and the post office. The house where he was born no longer

Water, water everywhere at Ely

exists but the church of **St Mary the Virgin**, where Constable's parents are buried, is at the end of the village.

Flatford Mill, owned by Constable's father, is a fair walk down the hill towards the river. The young Constable worked here for a while until he began to paint full time. The mill is now a National Trust field studies centre.

Across the River Stour at this point, public footpaths lead to the village of **Dedham**, with its much-painted watermill and 15th-century church.

◆◆
ELY
Cambridgeshire

Before the fenland was reclaimed from the sea, Ely was originally an island – Eel island – and the spire of its cathedral was the only landmark for miles around this flat expanse of cereal-growing land. And indeed the **cathedral** is the reason that most people visit the town. Within the cathedral, the star attraction is the Octagon, a wooden octagonal lantern of a grandeur and beauty all the greater in contrast with the austere simplicity of the nave. The Octagon was put up in 1322 when the original tower collapsed and is generally reckoned to be a masterpiece of early building. The carved choir stall and the Lady Chapel are beautiful. Your entry charge goes towards the renovation of the cathedral. On Sundays, of course, entry is free.

◆◆
KING'S LYNN
Norfolk

An historic market town and port on the River Ouse. It is the river's presence in King's Lynn, with the wharves as a reminder of a long history of shipping and trade, which gives this town its special character.

It was called plain Lynn until Henry VIII granted it a charter to hold an additional market, meaning there are now two markets, on Tuesday and Saturday. King's Lynn took its royal connections seriously, and was the only borough in East Anglia to support the restoration of the crown after the British Civil War. Note the statue of Charles II above the entrance to the **Custom House**. Visit **St Margaret's Church** by the river and the **Guildhall**, where some of King John's lost treasure, recovered from the Wash, is on display in the Regalia Rooms.

Around King's Lynn, features to look out for include the great wool churches. The **Seven Churches of the Marshland** stand on land drained and reclaimed from the sea between Wisbech and King's Lynn, on tiny roads off the A47. These seven churches are built in Perpendicular and Early English style. The star is **St Peter** at Walpole, but not far behind come **Wisbech St Mary**, **St Clement** at Terrington, **St Margaret** at Clenchwarton, **St Mary** at West Walton, **St Edmund** at Emneth and **All Saints** at Walsoken. North of King's Lynn, the seaside town of **Hunstanton** offers grand views of the Wash. **Holkham Hall** at Holkham, a Palladian mansion set in bare flat land, was the opulent home of Thomas Coke, Earl of Leicester.

Sandringham continues the Royal connection. **Sandringham House** is traditionally the spot where the Royal family spends Christmas, and where Queen Alexandra, and Kings George V and VI died. The house is open to the public when the family are not in residence, as are the parks and gardens.

◆◆
LAVENHAM
Suffolk

If you want to see a well preserved medieval wool town, Lavenham is it. The centre of the town lies between the great church of **St Peter and St Paul** on one hill and the **Market Square** and the **Guildhall** on the other.

The **Benedictine Priory**, dissolved by Henry VIII, is now in private hands and in the process of restoration. The **Swan Hotel** opposite is the place to have your tea. The oldest parts of this building date from the 14th century but evidence of more recent history can be found on the walls of the Old Bar, which bears the closely written signatures of members of the RAF, the USAF and the Army. Although his signature does not appear, it is said that the band leader Glenn Miller took his last drink here before he set off on his final tragic flight. In the pretty nearby village of **Kersey** thatched houses with mullioned windows, tumbling with geraniums, lean tipsily against each other down one hill and up another. A stream at the bottom of the dip often overflows. Drive carefully. Local residents are enraged by motorists who do not stop to let the ducks cross.

◆◆
LINCOLN
Lincolnshire
Tourists have not yet
discovered Lincoln to the same
degree as Lavenham, which is
strange, considering that this is
the site of one of Britain's
grandest cathedrals. The
cathedral stands on the crest
of a ridge rising high above
the plateau occupied by the
lower town and the River
Witham. Arriving from the
south, visitors enter the lower
town, crossing the river by the
12th-century **High Bridge**, then
making their way towards the
cathedral by ancient streets
which soon rise steeply
upwards in a manner that is
definitely un-East Anglian. Two
medieval houses on the way –
one known as the **Jew's House**,
the other as the **House of
Aaron** – testify to the
importance of the Jewish
community in medieval
business life. Occupying the
crest are the castle and
cathedral, both standing within
the precincts of the old Roman
settlement of *Lindum Colonia*,
the Colony of Lindum. The
castle has fine views and a
mixed interior, part medieval,
part 19th-century. The
cathedral, triple-towered and
grey-gold in colour, is the real
star, with a grandiloquent if
slightly ruinous west façade.
Built by the Normans,
damaged by an earthquake
and progressively
reconstructed in the 12th, 13th
and 14th centuries, this great
church gives an impression of
loftiness all the more dramatic
for being in this flat country.

Lincoln's castle and cathedral

◆
LOWESTOFT
Suffolk
This is as far east as you can
go in Britain. An important,
busy port, not just for catching
fish but for freezing and
processing them as well. Here,
they build the trawlers that go
out to the fishing fields and it
was here, too, that they built
Richard Branson's boat *Virgin
Atlantic Challenger II*.
Lowestoft is also a support
town for the North Sea oil
fields. Its maritime districts
offer plenty for the visitor, with
guided tours of the fish market
and docks. The pace is much
more leisurely in the centre of
town, which is old, with narrow,
winding streets. The beaches
are wide and sandy, but
northwards the coastline

changes into dunes. Those who want more up-to-date amusement can find it at **Pleasurewood Hills**, an American-style theme park, north of Lowestoft.

◆
NEWMARKET
Suffolk
This extremely agreeable town has been a horse-racing centre since the days of Charles II and is the home of the Jockey Club, which controls all racing activities in England.
The season runs from April to October and early in the morning you can see strings of horses being exercised for miles around the town. Look out for the house of Nell Gwynne, mistress of Charles II.

◆◆
NORWICH
Norfolk
An ancient, long-settled town whose early wealth was established through trading in wool and cloth with the Low Countries. The **Market Place**, still the scene of Britain's largest open air market, remains the focus of the town. Here is **St Peter Mancroft** church, built in the 1430s and famous for its stained-glass windows and Flemish tapestry. The **Guildhall** stands at the other end of Market Place with the 1930s **City Hall** occupying a third side of the square. There are over 30 medieval churches within the boundaries of the city, some now deconsecrated and used as museums. The great **cathedral**, with its beautiful

cloisters, is the finest of them all. It was originally built in 1096 and restored in the reign of Edward I. Edith Cavell, the nurse who was shot in Belgium for helping prisoners escape during World War I, is buried here. Norwich also has a 12th-century **castle**. Its museum houses work by the Norwich School landscape painters of the early 19th century and the American Memorial Library. Outside Norwich, the **Sainsbury Centre for Visual Arts**, on the campus of the University of East Anglia, has a formidable collection of modern, ancient, classical, medieval and ethnographic art, not to mention the Anderson collection of Art Nouveau and the university collection of Constructivist art. The Centre is an important modern building in its own right.

The heirlooms of Audley End House

◆
SAFFRON WALDEN
Essex
This pretty little town takes the name 'Saffron' from the yellow crocus. The **High Street** has fine examples of pargeting – decorated plaster facing on timber frame houses. To see the largest Jacobean house in England, visit nearby **Audley End**, owned on and off over the centuries by the Howard family.

◆
SUDBURY
Suffolk
This is a most attractive wool town, with green slopes down to the River Stour and surrounded on three sides by meadows. The artist Thomas Gainsborough was born here and his house is now a museum. Outside **St Gregory's Church**, at the top of the hill, a plain dark stone war memorial records the death of

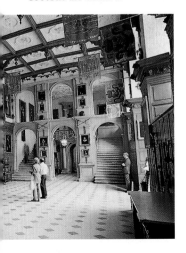

400 airmen, members of the 486 Bombardment Group. From Sudbury you can walk along the path of a disused railway to the town of **Long Melford** – 'Long' because the High Street runs for almost two miles (3km). As the shops peter out, the road rises between a long green on the left and the walled grounds of a red brick Elizabethan house – **Long Melford Hall** – on the right. The **Holy Trinity Church**, at the top of the hill, is a finely decorated wool church.

Accommodation

Aldeburgh
The **White Lion**, Market Cross Place (tel: (0728) 452720), is in an attractive position on the sea front. The popular restaurant serves fresh, well-prepared food in a relaxed atmosphere. Comfortable, inviting public areas and good service from a particularly friendly team of staff are among the special features of the **Brudenell**, The Parade (tel: (0728) 452071). **The Uplands**, Victoria Road (tel: (0728) 452420), on the approach road to town, provides neat, tidy accommodation.

Cambridge
The **Gonville**, Gonville Place (tel: (0223) 66611), offers spotless accommodation and high standards. **Arundel House**, at 53 Chesterton Road (tel: (0223) 67701) is comfortable and well-equipped. The **Post House**, Bridge Road (tel: (0223) 237000), has a

business centre and a health and leisure club.

Lincoln

The **Eastgate Post House**, Eastgate (tel: (0522) 520341) has well-equipped rooms and an interesting menu in the Palatinate Restaurant. Situated close to the castle, the **Duke William Hotel**, 44 Bailgate (tel: (0522) 533351) has friendly staff and a popular public bar and restaurant. **The Castle** in Westgate (tel: (0522) 38801) offers simply furnished bedrooms with a range of modern facilities.

Norwich

The Maid's Head, Tombland (tel: (0603) 761111) is an historic hotel with 13th-century features, in the shadow of the cathedral. **The Oaklands** overlooks the River Yare at 89 Yarmouth Road (tel: (0603) 34471). It offers good quality accommodation and a range of dishes. **Hotel Nelson**, in Prince of Wales Road (tel: (0603) 760260) has a choice of bar and restaurants.

Restaurants

Cambridge

Midsummer House, Midsummer Common (tel: (0223) 69299) comprises a series of small dining areas and has imaginative dishes.

Norwich

Marco's, 17 Pottergate (tel: (0603) 624044), is a popular little restaurant serving Italian dishes. **Greens Seafood**, at 82 Upper St Giles Street (tel: (0603) 623733) offers a wide variety of fish dishes.

MIDDLE ENGLAND

Middle England rose to comfort and prosperity on wool, was the birthplace of William Shakespeare, and went on to become the forge and anvil of the Industrial Revolution. Parts have never been touched by industry and remain deeply rural, full of tranquillity and an immemorial sense of settlement. Parts became a wilderness of smoke and factory and are only now re-emerging to find a new post-industrial identity.

Coming northwest out of London in the general direction of Oxford and Stratford, the traveller might first visit some of the little towns along the Thames – **Marlow**, **Wallingford** or **Henley**, for example. **The Chilterns**, a range of pleasant hills, now cross the way diagonally, offering such agreeable towns as **Aylesbury**. And then it is out across a wider landscape to **Oxford** and on to the old wool country of the **Cotswolds**, rich in towns and villages of warm and dusty-golden stone.

Shakespeare country lies just to the north, keeping close company with **Warwick** and **Kenilworth** and leading on to **Coventry**; and there are elegant spa towns as well, such as **Cheltenham** and **Leamington**.

For the independent traveller it is well worth carrying on as far as the triangle of cathedral cities, **Worcester**, **Hereford** and **Gloucester**, and the hill spa of **Malvern**, even, if possible, pushing on again into the deeply rural lands that lie along the border with Wales: **Herefordshire**, with its white villages like **Weobley**, **Eardisland** and **Pembridge**; and, north of Hereford, **Shropshire** and the heart of the Welsh Marches, with ruined Norman castles and a series of beautiful towns, chief among them **Ludlow** and **Shrewsbury**. Still further to the north, the border flattens out to the rich parkland of **Cheshire**.

The journey so far has produced a right-angle, from London straight across to the Welsh Border and then due north to Chester. Draw a line from Chester down to London to complete the triangle and the empty space not visited so far corresponds neatly to the site of the Industrial Revolution. This began, so we are told, along the River Severn in the **Gorge of Ironbridge**. At the start of the 19th century, activity moved on to **Stoke-on-Trent**, to the **Staffordshire** countryside (soon renamed the Black Country), and above all to **Birmingham**. In terms of population, Birmingham is Britain's second city, but it seems at first a messy, graceless place of buzzing overpasses and soulless underpasses. There are certainly no obvious reasons for tourists to visit Birmingham but those who do will begin to discover that this city is still marked by the active, individual character which made it Britain's leading place of manufacture. Passers-by should visit, if they can, the

Hereford Cathedral by the River Wye

City Museum and Art Gallery in Victoria Square for its collection of Pre-Raphaelite paintings, and the **Museum of Science and Industry** in Newhall Street for exhibits of early steam engines.

North of Birmingham is the rugged **Peak District** and finally, to complete the journey, travel south again to London through **Nottingham** (with Sherwood Forest and its legends of Robin Hood), through **Leicester**, then **Northampton** and **Bedfordshire**. The cities here lack appeal, but the quiet beauty of countryside and village, and of some of the market towns, still illustrates the best of ancient Middle England.

WHAT TO SEE

◆◆

BLENHEIM PALACE
Woodstock, Oxfordshire
Eight miles (13km) north of
Oxford, this great baroque
house was a gift to John
Churchill, Duke of
Marlborough, from Queen
Anne in 1704. It was named
after his first battle in the War
of Spanish Succession, against
the French at Blenheim.
No expense was spared
during the 28 years it took to
complete the 200-room
house. Sir John Vanbrugh and
Nicholas Hawksmoor were the
architects, Grinling

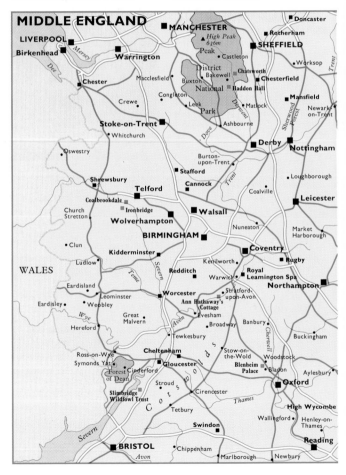

Gibbons was responsible for the wood carving and Capability Brown designed the 2,000 acres (810 hectares) of parkland around the house; the river was dammed to create a lake and trees were planted in the battle lines of the actual engagement.
Most people come here to see

the room where Sir Winston Churchill was born, prematurely, in 1874, while his mother was a house guest. There is also a small museum of his personal belongings. A short distance south of the palace lies the village of **Bladon** and the churchyard in which Churchill and his family are buried.
The lovely town of **Woodstock** brings you gently back to earth after the baroque heights of the palace.

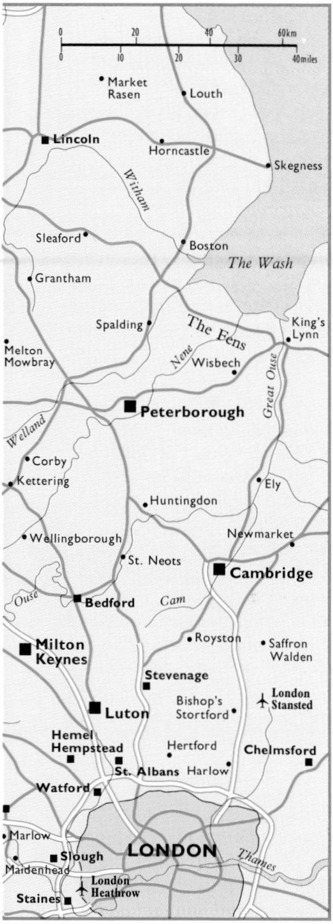

◆◆
CHESTER
Cheshire
Ringed by walls part medieval and part Roman, Chester is famous for its black and white, half-timbered buildings. Their high black gables and heavily overhanging upper storeys, dense with timber patterning against the white of plaster, seem the very quintessence of Old English style. The curious fact, however, is that many of the finest façades are late Victorian reconstructions.
A major Roman city, heavily fortified and with a large-scale port on the River Dee, Chester was laid out in a long rectangle reaching back from the river. It remained a major harbour during the Middle Ages, exporting gloves and candles, salt and cheese. Finally the river silted up and today the former harbour has become the Roodee racecourse, immediately adjacent to the city walls.
The whole of the two-mile (3km) circuit of the walls can still be made on foot, offering

in order (starting westwards from Northgate Street): views of the **old city** within, the **River Dee**, the **Eastgate clock**, said to be the most photographed timepiece in Britain after London's Big Ben, the **cathedral**, unexceptional except for the carved misericords in the choir stalls, and finally **King Charles's Tower**, from which Charles I watched the defeat of his forces during the Civil War. In the city centre are the **Chester Rows**. These are elevated arcades at first floor level, set back behind the façades and running across the front of many buildings, often of different age and style, with a second tier of shops inside them. The top streets for architecture are **Bridge Street** and **Watergate Street**. See also the **Bear and Billet** public house in Lower Bridge Street, former home of the Earls of Shrewsbury.

THE COTSWOLDS

Evesham • Mickleton •
Hidcote Manor • Shipston-on-Stour •
Broadway • Chipping Campden
Buckland • Batsford Arboretum
Stanton • Snowshill • Moreton-in-Marsh
Snowshill Manor
Stanway
• Winchcombe
Sudeley Castle • Stow-on-the-Wold
Upper Slaughter • Kingham •
• Lower Slaughter
• Bourton-on-the-Water
• Shipton
Windrush
Northleach •
0   5   10km
0   5miles
Burford •

◆◆◆
THE COTSWOLDS
The Lord Chancellor (who is speaker of the House of Lords) still sits on the 'woolsack' – such is the enduring symbolism of the sheep as the source of English prosperity. And in its day – that is to say, from the 12th to 15th centuries – there was no region more prosperous than this high rolling plateau between the Thames and Severn river basins. Merchants raised armies of Cotswold Lion sheep and spent their wealth on grand houses and churches in pale golden stone.
Bourton-on-the-Water, Gloucestershire, is picturesque, if you like crowd scenes. The shallow Windrush river flows through the centre of this town, with toy-sized footbridges connecting one side to the other. Diversions include the **perfumery**, the **motorcar museum**, various craft shops and the **model village**, a miniature version of Bourton in Cotswold stone. There are many lesser known but no less attractive places. **Snowshill**, for example, just a couple of miles south of busy Broadway, is an enchanting little village tumbling down a hillside with cosy pubs and a Tudor manor house. **Upper and Lower Slaughter** are two villages which have everything – fine houses, cottages, fords, footbridges and mills.
A marked trail of about 100 miles (160km) of footpaths leads you through the **Cotswold Way**. Details from local Tourist Information Centres.

Cotswolds charm: Lower Slaughter

Chipping Campden – the word 'chipping' means 'market' – was the centre of the Cotswold wool trade. The town nestles at the foot of a hill edged by a handful of thatched houses. Wealthy merchants lived in the fine high gabled houses along the High Street. Look out for the **Market Hall**, the **Woolstapler's Hall** and **William Grevel's House**, both 14th-century buildings, and the almshouses. The focus of **Stow-on-the-Wold**, Gloucestershire, the highest town in the Cotswolds, remains the market square. An ancient market cross stands at one end and at the other, wooden stocks on a small green. This is now an affluent town of antiques and interior design shops. The **Church of St Edward** is where Oliver Cromwell held a company of Royalists during the 17th-century Civil War, then shot a few of them.

◆

COVENTRY
West Midlands

Coventry was the centre of munitions production during World War II and, inevitably, the target of German bombing raids during which much of the old city was destroyed. The rebuilt Coventry is, like any other modern city, given over to pedestrianised shopping precincts and office blocks. There are two outstanding features. The first is the legend of Lady Godiva, who lived in the 11th century. As her part of the bargain in persuading her husband Leofric to rescind an unpopular tax, she had to ride through the town naked. The citizens of Coventry, full of sympathetic gratitude, resolutely stayed behind doors and refused to look as she passed – except Peeping Tom. Anyone can look now: a bronze statue of Lady Godiva on her horse stands outside the new shopping precinct on Broadgate in the city centre. The other great feature is the **cathedral**, or rather the two cathedrals. The new one, mottled pink in red sandstone, rises out of the bombed and blackened ruins of the original 14th-century structure. It was designed by Sir Basil Spence and dedicated in 1962. Epstein's last work, *St Michael triumphant over the Devil*, stands against the wall as you enter. The stained glass window in the baptistery was designed by John Piper, and Graham Sutherland designed the tapestry of *Christ in Glory* behind the altar. The view back along the nave of the church is of figures of angels, leaping and soaring against the background of the old cathedral spire, incised on the huge glass screen by John Hutton. The Coventry Mystery Plays are performed among the ruins of the old cathedral each summer.

Coventry was an important centre of the cloth industry until the 17th century and there are some fine old buildings to show for it. Look out for **Holy Trinity Church**, **St Mary's Hall**, and **Ford's Hospital** and **Bond's Hospital**, two 16th-century poorhouses. In the Tourist Information Centre (opposite the cathedral), medieval cellars have been discovered. Previously scattered medieval buildings have been transplanted to **Spon Street**, where they form a small nucleus of Old Coventry.

◆
GLOUCESTER
Gloucestershire

Gloucester has not benefited from ugly 20th-century building. But a visit is well justified by the cathedral, and by the massive 19th-century docks, strange to encounter so far inland, and recently refurbished.

The **cathedral**, set in a harmonious and restful close, is basically a Norman construction set inside Perpendicular cladding. The 15th-century tower is particularly delightful from a distance, and the early fan vaulting of the cloisters, though low, is sumptuous and elaborate. The cathedral houses the tomb of the murdered King Edward II.

The **Gloucester Docks** are a great surprise, huge basins of water surrounded by six-storey warehouses profuse in windows. One houses the **Gloucester Antiques Centre**.

◆◆
HEREFORD
Hereford and Worcester
High Town, the old market centre, is today an example of injudicious rebuilding and the power of bank and chain store logos. But as with Gloucester, it is the **cathedral**, here in soft and reddish sandstone, which compels a visit.

Architecturally the building is a mixture, with Norman tower and nave, an Early English crypt and Lady Chapel. The tower is in Decorated style. Its two great treasures are a library of chained books and manuscripts and the 13th-century World Map, or *Mappa Mundi*, which the cathedral authorities lately attempted to sell. General outrage halted the transaction. Beware, though – while the cathedral is open to the public throughout the day, the library and *Mappa Mundi* are visible only

The original Iron Bridge

for short periods.
Bulmers, the local cider manufacturers, have a **Cider Museum** on the west side of town.

◆◆
IRONBRIDGE/ COALBROOKDALE
Shropshire
It is said that the Industrial Revolution began in the early 18th century in a narrow defile of the River Severn, where the river flowed swiftly south between the Welsh border and the settlement which later became Birmingham. There were forests for charcoal, together with outcropping coal and iron-ore right in the valley. The river was still navigable and products could be easily exported. Here the Shropshire Iron Masters set up shop, initiating a frenzy of activity. As an advertisement for their wares they built, at Ironbridge, the world's first wrought-iron bridge. Soon the valley was turning out iron rails and wheels, iron boats, even the first high pressure steam locomotive. Coalport china was also made here.
The valley, once beautiful, became a smoky warren of furnaces and kilns, canals coming in at different levels, with a host of open pit shafts, enormous wealth and considerable misery. By 1810 it was all over. The Severn ceased to be navigable and as a result, the Industrial Revolution moved on to other parts of the country. Forests grew again in the Ironbridge gorge.

It is only in recent years that the industrial sites have been reclaimed, and many of them reopened, over an area of six square miles (15 sq km), as a single enterprise – the **Ironbridge Gorge Museum**. The place to start is the **Museum of the River and Visitor Centre** in Ironbridge. The museums may either be visited singly or on a general 'passport', allowing entry to all sites and on different occasions.

◆◆
LUDLOW
Shropshire
Ludlow is a charming border town, remarkably unspoilt, with a mighty castle, handsome streets of medieval, Tudor, Jacobean and Georgian houses and a lofty Perpendicular parish church which could do duty as a cathedral. The **castle**, which witnessed the first performance of Milton's masque *Comus*, is on a dominant outcrop above the River Teme. It played a major part in holding and administering the border and gave its hospitality to many royal visitors.

The oldest part of town, with market square and church, and fine black and white houses, runs back from the castle along a high spur of land. Wide streets, mostly Georgian, run up towards the tight little tangle at the top. **The Feathers** pub, close to the top, is one of the most ornately carved and decorated of England's half-timbered buildings.

◆◆◆
OXFORD
Oxfordshire
After a visit to Oxford, the 19th-century American novelist Henry James felt that his heart 'would crack with satisfied desire'. This is not a universal response, but Oxford, like Cambridge, brings out the hyperbole in many visitors. What these university towns have in common is the weight of history and of academic prestige as well as the beauty of ancient buildings in lovely landscape – all within the distance of a short walk. Oxford began its history in 1167, a little earlier than Cambridge. As a town known for car manufacture as well for its university, there is a stronger connection here than in Cambridge between 'town and gown'.

The aim of most visitors is to see the individual colleges which make up the university. Many colleges lead off the High Street, known as '**The High**'. Like fashionable London clubs they do nothing to identify themselves. As you arrive in town, head straight for the Tourist Information Office on St Aldates, just south of the **Carfax Tower**, the virtual hub of Oxford, to pick up essential maps, or book a walking tour. If you elect to discover the colleges independently, a short list of those you should not miss would include **Christ Church**, founded by Cardinal Wolsey in 1525. This college is famous for its great picture gallery, including works of the Italian, Dutch and Flemish schools, and its chapel, gardens and meadow running down to the River Isis – as the Thames is called at this point. If you are there at 9:05P.M. during the term, you will hear Great Tom, the huge bell in the tower of the quad, which tolls 101 times, once for each of the original members of the college. Christ Church has produced 13 prime ministers and 20 archbishops. C L Dodgson, alias Lewis Carroll, author of *Alice in Wonderland*, was also a member.

Merton College, near by, was founded in 1264. Some argument remains over whether it can be described as the oldest college although it has the oldest library and the oldest chapel.

The poet Shelley was a member of **University College**, and his memorial is to your right as you enter. Poor cold, marble Shelley lies on a bier in a starry, blue-domed room. The memorial was installed here at his widow's request: an odd site, since Shelley was never a model student – indeed, he was expelled from the university for publishing an atheistic tract (enquire at Porter's Lodge for permission to see the memorial).

Magdalen College, pronounced 'Maudlin', stands beside the River Cherwell. Oscar Wilde was an undergraduate here. The 100-acre (40-hectare) grounds, with deer park, meadows and riverside walks, make it idyllic. The Magdalen tradition is that the chapel choir climbs the tower of the college at

Carfax clocktower

6:00A.M. on 1 May every year for a dawn chorus of madrigals.

Other major sights in Oxford include the **Radcliffe Camera** and the **Bodleian Library**; the **Sheldonian Theatre**, designed by Christopher Wren; and the **Ashmolean Museum**, housing the great art and archaeological treasures of the university. Opposite Balliol College is the **Martyrs' Memorial**, where the Protestant bishops Cranmer, Latimer and Ridley, were burned at the stake in the reign of Mary Tudor.

A traditional Oxford experience for every visitor is to rent a punt for the afternoon. Punting is harder than it looks. If you have to choose between parting company with your punt or your pole, as you drift down the river, stay with the punt.

The Peak District

◆◆
PEAK DISTRICT

One of the least touched parts of England, the Peak District is ringed by the cities of Sheffield and Manchester, Stoke-on-Trent and Derby. The main beauty spots can be uncomfortably crowded on summer Sundays, but it is still easy to escape on to wild hills and to find a refuge in remoter valleys. The southern half of the Peak District consists mainly of green farmland, scored by deep and highly picturesque gorges. The northern half is mostly moorland, often bleak. North and south alike are remarkable for the beauty of their valleys, with rivers like the Derwent and the Wye providing sites for handsome stone villages and towns and majestic country houses.

Ashbourne, Derbyshire, has some pleasant Georgian houses and one of the few remaining English pub signs which stretch right across the street. It is the most obvious point of access for the southern part of the **Peak District National Park**, notably **Dove Dale** and its tight-pressing gorge. The village of **Tissington**, near by, is mostly 19th-century and totally unspoilt. It is believed to have been the starting place, in the Middle Ages, of the local practice of well-dressing. Large pictures of biblical scenes, done in petals and greenery, are inlaid into soft clay frames which are erected over wells as a devotional gesture.

Bakewell, Derbyshire, with its five-arched bridge across the River Wye, is a pretty stone town, once important for its markets. It is famous for its pudding, a soft compound of batter and strawberry jam, and famous too for Bakewell tart, a custard pastry now mass-produced. The fine medieval house of **Haddon Hall** rises above the River Wye in the immediate vicinity.

Buxton, Derbyshire, is a remarkable and gracious spa town, set in steep up-and-down countryside 1,000 feet (305m) above sea-level. Its domes and turrets, stone-built row houses and crescents are, though on a smaller scale, a genuine rival to Bath (see page 94).

Castleton, Derbyshire, in the Hope Valley, ranks with Dove Dale as a summer attraction. It has a fine situation, with a steep green crag above, surmounted by the ruins of **Peveril Castle**. There are a number of show caves in the district, notably **Blue John Cavern**. Most caves are associated with the mining of Blue John, a semi-precious feldspar.

Chatsworth, seat of the Dukes of Devonshire, is just a few miles from Bakewell. It rises in grandeur above the meadows of the Derwent, with steep and wooded hills behind. It was rebuilt in its present form by the architect William Talman from the 1680s on, and an extra wing was built in the 1820s. Chatsworth is one of the most palatial country houses in Britain, both architecturally and in its art collections and gardens. The gardens are notable for a formal cascade that comes tumbling down the hill, for astonishingly powerful gravity-fed fountains and for the orangery.

Edale, Derbyshire, marks the start of the 250-mile (402km) Pennine Way.

◆◆
SHREWSBURY
Shropshire

Shropshire's county town is one of the most substantial cities on the English side of the Welsh border. It rises on a hump of hill which is itself almost completely surrounded by a loop of the River Severn: a place of medieval passageways and alleys, of buried courtyards and big calm churchyards, set around a series of impressive churches. Look at the sandstone **castle**, (now a dwelling place), **St Mary's Church** and the **Abbey Church** (the latter on the far side of the river). But this is as fine a city as any for simply wandering about. The town's border position is symbolised by the names of the two of its main bridges, the **Welsh Bridge** and the **English Bridge**.

MIDDLE ENGLAND

##
STOKE-ON-TRENT
Staffordshire
Stoke-on-Trent is a conurbation consisting of six towns: Burslem, Hanley, Fenton, Longton, Tunstall and Stoke itself. Lying a little north of Birmingham and the Black Country, it is dreary to look at, but fascinating to anyone with even a passing interest in china. This is the home of Wedgwood, Minton, Royal Doulton, Masons and Spode. Right up until the 1950s, the porcelain was baked in coal-fired kilns, making the Six Towns a smoky inferno. Following the Clean Air Act, the kilns were replaced by gas-fired ovens, creating a dramatic change in the atmosphere. Some 40 of the factory shops can be visited, and factory tours are offered by several famous names. (**Wedgwood**, with an excellent visitors' centre and museum, has been resited a few miles from Stoke.) The **Stoke-on-Trent Museum** has one of the world's better china displays. The geography of the area is complicated, making it rather hard to visit independently. But 'The China Service' has buses running in continuous loops through five Potteries towns and the Wedgwood site, starting from Stoke railway station and stopping at all the main points of interest.

##
STRATFORD-UPON-AVON
Warwickshire
This whole town is a virtual shrine to William Shakespeare.

He was born here in 1564, returned here from London as a wealthy and famous playwright, and died here in 1616. Not surprisingly, Stratford is full of the monuments of his life. The pilgrimage to the town gathered momentum after the first Shakespeare Festival, organised by the actor David Garrick, in 1769.
Shakespeare's birthplace is in Henley Street on the hill above the river. The house is entered by way of the **Shakespeare Centre**, which displays costumes used in BBC productions of his plays. Visitors are carefully routed to the house itself, fragrant with beeswax and traditional pot-pourri. The first floor bedroom, with a tiny cradle beside the double bed, is reputedly 'the' birthplace.
The foundations are all that is visible of the house that Shakespeare bought for himself as an adult in **New Place**. It is said that an 18th-century owner of the house was so enraged by the number of Shakespeare fans hunting souvenirs that he burned it down. There is, though, a most attractive Elizabethan 'knot' garden and a large flower garden behind. At least **Nash House**, which once belonged to Shakespeare's granddaughter, still stands intact next door. It is now a museum.
On the opposite side of the High Street, the grand half-timbered **Harvard House** was the family home of John Harvard, founder of Harvard

University.
Hall's Croft, further down the
street and round the corner in
Old Town, belonged to
Shakespeare's daughter
Susannah and her husband, Dr
John Hall. Shakespeare is
buried with other members of
his family in the chancel of the
Holy Trinity Church, under a
simple stone tablet. A wreath
is laid here on 23 April each
year, the anniversary of both
his birth and death.
Most people agree that the
best living monument to the
genius of Shakespeare is the
presence of the **Royal
Shakespeare Company**,
performing the whole cycle of
the master's plays in a
purpose-built theatre on the
banks of the Avon. The season
runs from March to January;
reserve ahead if you want
tickets in the summer. There
are regular backstage tours.
The **Swan Theatre** stages the
work of playwrights
contemporary with and
following Shakespeare, and
you can see modern work in
The Other Place.
Other Shakespeare
monuments include the **cottage**
of his wife, Anne Hathaway,
just outside the town of
Shottery, one mile (1.6km) west
of Stratford. This old two-storey
thatched-roof farm house was
owned and occupied until 1899
by members of the family and
contains some original
furniture. A worm-eaten settle
in the kitchen is reputedly
where William and Anne did
their courting. Reverential
guides may allow you to sit
down on it.

Anne Hathaway's cottage

◆◆
WARWICK
Warwickshire
The showpiece **castle** here
was built by William the
Conqueror and was the home
of the Earls of Warwick. Its
fortifications have not changed
much since the 14th century,
although the interior was
largely restored in 1871 after a
fire. The castle was sold in
1978 to the owners of Madame
Tussaud's Waxworks, and has
been successfully packaged
for the tourist market. A royal
weekend party of 1898 has
been recreated on the basis of
photographs and other
records, using waxwork
models, contemporary
costumes and furniture.
The State Apartments are rich
with fine furniture and
paintings, including a portrait
of Charles I by Van Dyck. The
Great Hall jangles with

weapons and armour, and the death mask of Oliver Cromwell shows him peaceful at last. There is also a haunted tower, torture chambers, beautiful grounds, calling peacocks, and the River Avon winding past the castle. Much of Warwick was destroyed in a fire in 1694 but there is still some fine 17th- and 18th-century building. Nearby, at **Kenilworth**, the magnificent ruins of a vast red sandstone castle are another romantic diversion: this was a gift from Queen Elizabeth I to her favourite, Robert Dudley, Earl of Leicester.

◆
WORCESTER
Hereford and Worcester
Worcester Cathedral makes a trinity with those of Gloucester and Hereford (the Three Choirs Festival is held in one of them each year). In Worcester, the cathedral rises majestically above the Severn, turning its west end towards the river. It began its days as a monastery church and here King John was buried at his own request. His tomb (1230), right in the centre beneath the high altar, carries the earliest effigy of an English king. The traffic swirls horribly close to the east end of the cathedral, but it is worth walking into the close on the far side, a place of great beauty.
There are a few old streets, particularly **Fish Street** and the pedestrian **Friars Street**, and there are good riverside walks on the far side of the river. In the High Street, note the handsome brick and stone 17th-century **Guildhall**. The Royal Worcester porcelain company has a **museum**, and offers tours of the works.

Accommodation
Chester
The recently refurbished **Chester Grosvenor**, Eastgate Street (tel: (0244) 324024) offers excellent accommodation and a fine restaurant. **Blossoms**, in St John Street (tel: (0244) 323186), in the city centre, is ideal for the tourist, and **The Green Bough**, 60 Hoole Road (tel: (0244) 326241), is a warm and friendly hotel which provides an intimate restaurant.

The Cotswolds
The **Old Manse** in Victoria Street, **Bourton-on-the-Water**, (tel: (0451) 20082) offers refurbished accommodation with modern facilities.

Worcester's exuberant Guildhall

Bedrooms are individually designed and decorated in the **Cotswold House Hotel**, The Square, **Chipping Campden** (tel: (0386) 840330). Imaginative cuisine is served in the charming dining room. The **Unicorn Crest**, Sheep Street, **Stow-on-the-Wold** (tel: (0451) 30257), is a pleasant hotel offering a range of *en suite* rooms. Also in Sheep Street, the **Grapevine** (tel: (0451) 30344) has a relaxed and informal atmosphere.

Oxford
Linton Lodge, Linton Road (tel: (0865) 53461) offers a blend of modern and traditional well-equipped accommodation. Close to the station, the **Royal Oxford**, Park End Street (tel: (0865) 248432) provides bright, modern bedrooms and a small restaurant. The **Eastgate Hotel**, Merton Street (tel: (0865) 248244) in the heart of the city, is elegantly

furnished with a hot buffet restaurant and student bar. Rooms range from the sumptuous to the modest.

The Peak District
The **Beresford Arms** in Station Road, **Ashbourne** (tel: (0335) 300035) is a fully renovated hotel with tastefully furnished rooms. The **Palace Hotel** in Palace Road, **Buxton** (tel: (0298) 22001) overlooks the spa town and provides recently upgraded accommodation, a gymnasium and swimming pool.

Stratford-upon-Avon
The **Grosvenor House Hotel** in Warwick Road (tel: (0789) 269213) has 51 bedrooms, many refurbished to high standards. A health centre is now an added attraction. The **Swan's Nest**, Bridgefoot (tel: (0789) 66761) offers guests comfortable bedrooms and a choice of menus. The **Stratford House Hotel** in Sheep Street (tel: (0789) 68288) has a reputation for excellent modern British cooking.

Restaurants
Oxford
Restaurant Elizabeth, in St Aldates (tel: (0865) 242230), has a short but interesting menu offering French, Spanish and Greek cuisine. **Gees** is a bistro restaurant in Banbury Road (tel: (0865) 53540) providing friendly, informal service. At the **Paddyfield**, 39-40 Hythe Bridge Street (tel: (0865) 248835) well-prepared, authentic Cantonese and Pekinese dishes are offered.

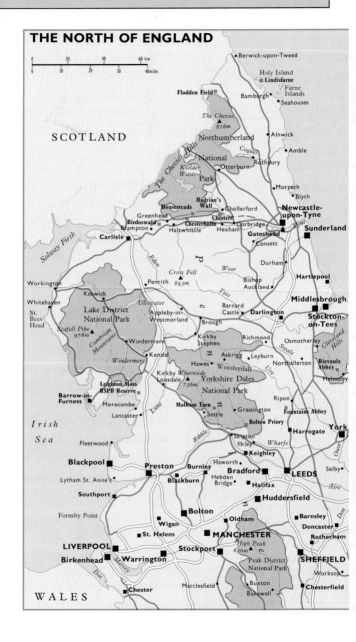

THE NORTH OF ENGLAND

0   20   40   60 km
0   10   20   30   40 miles

• Berwick-upon-Tweed

Holy Island
▪ Lindisfarne
Farne
Islands

Flodden Field •
Bamburgh •
• Seahouses

The Cheviot
816m

SCOTLAND

Northumberland
• Alnwick

The Cheviot Hills
Coquet
• Amble

National
Rothbury
• Otterburn

Kielder
Water
Park
• Morpeth

Hadrian's
Wall
• Blyth

Housesteads
Greenhead
• Chollerford
Newcastle-
upon-Tyne

Birdoswald
Chesters
Corbridge

Brampton
Chesterholm
Hexham
Gateshead
Sunderland

Haltwhistle
Tyne

Carlisle
Consett

Solway Firth
Eden
P
Wear
Durham •

Cross Fell
893m
Bishop
Auckland •
Hartlepool

Workington
• Penrith
Tees

Whitehaven
Keswick
Ullswater
Barnard
Castle
Darlington
Middlesbrough

St.
Bees
Head
Lake District
National Park
Appleby-in-
Westmorland
Richmond
Stockton-
on-Tees

Seafell Pike
978m
Brough
Osmotherley
Cleveland Hills

Cumbrian Mountains
Kirkby
Stephen
Askrigg
Leyburn
Northallerton
Rievaulx
Abbey

Windermere
Swale

Kendal
Hawes
Wensleydale
Ure
Helmsley

Windermere
Kirkby
Lonsdale
Whernside
736m
Yorkshire Dales

Leighton Moss
RSPB Reserve
National Park

Barrow-in-
Furness
Morecambe
Ripon

Lune
Malham Tarn
Grassington
Fountains Abbey

Lancaster
Settle
Bolton Priory
York

*Irish
Sea*
Ribble
Skipton
Harrogate

Ilkley
Wharfe

Fleetwood •
Keighley
Ouse

Selby

Blackpool
Preston
Burnley
Haworth
Bradford
LEEDS

Lytham St. Anne's •
Blackburn
Hebden
Bridge
Halifax
Aire

Southport
Huddersfield

Formby Point
Bolton

Wigan
Oldham
Barnsley
Doncaster

• St. Helens
MANCHESTER
Rotherham

LIVERPOOL
Stockport
High Peak
636m

Birkenhead
Warrington
SHEFFIELD

Mersey
Peak District
National Park
Worksop

Dee
Buxton
Chesterfield

WALES
Chester
Macclesfield
Bakewell

THE NORTH

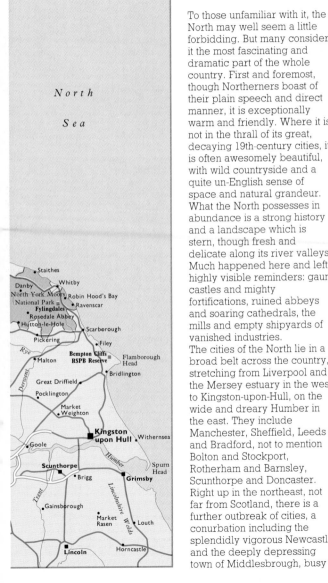

To those unfamiliar with it, the
North may well seem a little
forbidding. But many consider
it the most fascinating and
dramatic part of the whole
country. First and foremost,
though Northerners boast of
their plain speech and direct
manner, it is exceptionally
warm and friendly. Where it is
not in the thrall of its great,
decaying 19th-century cities, it
is often awesomely beautiful,
with wild countryside and a
quite un-English sense of
space and natural grandeur.
What the North possesses in
abundance is a strong history
and a landscape which is
stern, though fresh and
delicate along its river valleys.
Much happened here and left
highly visible reminders: gaunt
castles and mighty
fortifications, ruined abbeys
and soaring cathedrals, the
mills and empty shipyards of
vanished industries.
The cities of the North lie in a
broad belt across the country,
stretching from Liverpool and
the Mersey estuary in the west
to Kingston-upon-Hull, on the
wide and dreary Humber in
the east. They include
Manchester, Sheffield, Leeds
and Bradford, not to mention
Bolton and Stockport,
Rotherham and Barnsley,
Scunthorpe and Doncaster.
Right up in the northeast, not
far from Scotland, there is a
further outbreak of cities, a
conurbation including the
splendidly vigorous Newcastle
and the deeply depressing
town of Middlesbrough, busy

with the manufacture of chemicals.

Few tourists will seek out the Northern cities. Yet they must certainly be greeted with a salute. Liverpool, Manchester, Leeds and Newcastle are major cultural centres, with flourishing musical, theatrical and intellectual lives. Physically they are becoming rather more appealing as they start to remake themselves for a post-industrial age.

Liverpool, for instance, once known as the home of dereliction and dismay, has now refurbished its handsome 19th-century Albert Docks, establishing them as one of the country's leading visitor attractions – along with a modern tourism which takes in the Cavern Club and all the other now legendary haunts of the Beatles. Currently, however, it is **Manchester** which leads the way in pop music in Britain, making this city a Mecca among the young. Alongside the English population, particularly in Leeds and Bradford, there is a large Asian community. Manchester has a considerable black population, mainly from the Caribbean, while Liverpool, once second only to London as a port, has a substantial Chinese community, a black community descended mainly from African seafarers and more Irish citizens than most cities in the Irish Republic. The visitor who penetrates these urban societies will be rewarded with a richer, and perhaps a truer experience of England.

The Lie of the Land

The industrial cities of the Manchester-Sheffield belt are mostly separated from one another by high moorland. This is because the Pennine chain, the rugged backbone of England, originates in the Derby Peaks just to the south, and moves directly northwards, first through the industrial cities and then through open country virtually to the Scottish border. All the way up, there are other groups of hills to east and west, sometimes virtually part of the Pennines, sometimes separated by low country and farmland.

First, approximately central, come the **Yorkshire Dales** effectively within the Pennines. Almost at the same level, though well out to the east of the country, are the quite separate **North York Moors**. Still moving northwards, the next in order are the **Cumbrian Mountains**, the rugged and lovely high ground of the Lake District. **The Lakes** are in the west, occupying a lobe of land that is almost a peninsula. At the dead centre of the country come the green **Cheviot Hills**, right up on the Scottish border.

Each of these four groups of hills makes up the core of a national park. In south-to-north order, these are: the **Yorkshire Dales National Park**, the **North York Moors National Park**, the **Lake District National Park** and the **Northumberland National Park** (which includes the Cheviots). All offer splendid walking and outdoor pursuits.

WHAT TO SEE

◆◆◆
ABBEYS

Fountains Abbey ranks supreme among romantic ruins. Four miles (6km) southwest of Ripon, and some 21 miles (34km) from York, this impressive 12th-century Cistercian monastery, once the richest in all England, stands in the green and wooded valley of the River Skell. It is open to the skies but large parts of the walls are well preserved. The whole ground plan is easily recognisable. The nave of the church, with its 11 long bays, and the chapel of the Nine Altars are poignant reminders of a past glory.

The visitor has a sudden and magnificent view of Fountains from the gardens of **Studley Royal**. Seemingly artless, this was in fact a carefully contrived landscape on the part of Studley Royal's 18th-century owner. The stones of the Abbey were also used to build **Fountains Hall**.

Bolton Priory, on a loop of the River Wharfe in Wharfedale, is small in comparison. It is similarly ruined, with the exception of the Early English nave, spared during the Dissolution of the Monasteries which followed Henry VIII's break with Rome. The area north of the Priory is excellent for walking. Don't go too near the edge of Strid chasm, where the river rushes through a narrow gorge in Bolton woods.

Rievaulx Abbey (pronounced Reevo) is in Ryedale, a little way northwest of the town of Helmsley on the edge of the North York Moors National Park. This great Cistercian abbey, mostly in Early English style, was founded in 1132. Because of the narrowness of the valley, it was built on an unusual north-south axis. Still imposing in its ruined state, it dominates the village of honey-coloured cottages below. As at Fountains, there have been attempts to incorporate the ruins into a scheme of contrived landscape architecture. From a high terrace, graced by a couple of 18th-century Greek temples, visitors can enjoy a dramatic vista of the abbey below.

Deserted Fountains Abbey

THE NORTH

Berwick's Royal Border Bridge

♦♦♦
BERWICK-UPON-TWEED
Northumberland

The modern border between England and Scotland runs diagonally northeast from the Solway Firth to the mouth of the Tweed. Berwick stands on the north side of the Tweed in what should logically be Scotland. It was indeed Scottish in its early centuries, one of the wealthiest towns of Britain's northern kingdom. No wonder so rich a prize changed hands 13 times during the wars between Scots and English. Though it has since remained an English enclave on the wrong side of the river, it was always vulnerable and it was Queen Elizabeth I who ringed Berwick with mighty ramparts and bastions as a defence against cannon fire. Entering the city from the south by one of three dramatic bridges over the Tweed, the visitor will soon feel compelled to walk the ramparts, enjoying views down into the town and southwards along the line of the Northumbrian coast. The town itself has some of the most handsome Georgian architecture in England. There are two interesting museums. On the top floor of the 18th-century **Town Hall**, under a high steeple, the local jail has somehow survived intact. Higher up, in the northeast corner of the town, are Britain's first purpose-built **barracks** (1717–21). As well as a military museum the barracks hold a curious collection of artworks and artefacts.

Flodden Field, where the English devastated 'the flower of Scotland' in 1513, is about half-an-hour's drive southwest, in rolling, unspoiled countryside. Recommended.

◆◆
BRONTË COUNTRY or HAWORTH
West Yorkshire

Formerly a small stone village on the moors, Haworth has grown rapidly in recent years. In the summer the narrow, winding streets are full of visitors who come to pay homage to the town's most famous former inhabitants. Writers Charlotte, Emily and Anne Brontë, with their brother Branwell, spent most of their life in the parsonage at Haworth after their father took up his appointment here in 1820. The restored **Brontë Parsonage Museum** is at the top of the High Street on the edge of town, virtually where the moors begin. Family memorabilia include books, manuscripts and drawings. All the Brontës, except Anne, are buried in the family vault in the parish church next door. Beyond the churchyard, paths lead to distant open moorland. Various landmarks in this brooding landscape have been designated the likely models for places in the novels. Top Withins, a ruined farmhouse, is thought to be the basis for Emily's *Wuthering Heights*.

The **Black Bull** pub, from which the unfortunate Branwell used to stagger home to his three sisters, is still open for refreshment.

For those with a taste for steam, the **Worth Valley Steam Railway** runs a short trip between Keighley and Oxenhope with a stop at Haworth.

◆◆
CARLISLE
Cumbria

Carlisle's role as a border town is amply illustrated by exhibits at the **Tullie House Museum**, with a special emphasis on nearby Hadrian's Wall. The national wars between the English and Scots are well illustrated, as is the border fighting of the Rievers (or Raiders) who for centuries contested the so-called Debatable Lands north and east of Carlisle.

Across the road from Tullie House is **Carlisle Castle**, gloomy, red and low, heavily refortified by Henry VIII, who feared invasion by the Catholic Scots following his rejection of Rome.

The other main sight of Carlisle is its small, red stone **cathedral**, extended at one end after stone was pinched from the other for Henry VIII's castle improvements. It has excellent 15th-century misericords and, in its east window, one of England's finer displays of stained glass.

◆◆
DALES
Yorkshire

The Yorkshire Dales, a national park, are upland river valleys formed initially by the melting waters of the Ice Age. Barren, steep hillsides of bracken and heather, with sudden outcrops of rock, give way in lower slopes to green woods, with becks or streams falling to rivers below. Small, isolated farms, bounded by dry stone walls, cling to these hillsides. Villages nestle deep in the valleys. **Swaledale** is the most northerly and, in the opinion of many, the wildest and loveliest; **Wensleydale** is much visited by fans of James Herriot, the veterinary surgeon-turned-writer. His best-selling books about his veterinary practice in the Dales and the television series based on them have brought thousands of new visitors to this area, particularly to the town of **Askrigg**, where many of the scenes from *All Creatures Great and Small* were filmed. Although they are a pleasure to drive through, the Dales are the natural territory of climbers, underground cave explorers and walkers. Those who prefer to walk marked tracks are well served by the **Dales Way**, **Ribble Way** and **Pennine Way**.

♦♦♦
DURHAM
County Durham

Magnificent seems the only word for this small medieval city with its imposing castle and incomparable cathedral, located close together on a rocky outcrop surrounded on three sides by the River Wear. The old city itself is steep and attractive, with narrow lanes and ancient frontages, the whole given a touch of life by the presence of students from the 19th-century university.

The **cathedral** was built swiftly, between 1093 and 1133, with few alterations and additions, giving it an unusual unity of style. It is both seriously Norman and profusely decorated, within and without. The round internal arches are enlivened by fierce chevron patterns, while the massive columns are themselves decorated with deeply incised zigzags and double-sided diamonds. The tomb of St Cuthbert, once a major place of pilgrimage, lies in the east, behind the high altar, while at the other end of the cathedral the Venerable Bede, author of the earliest history of England, lies in the Galilee Chapel, an elegant construction with patches of medieval painting surviving high up.

The **castle**, seat of the bishops, is now largely occupied by the university. Kitchen, great hall and chapel are open to visitors.

Following the cobbled street from Durham's Norman castle, you reach the market place and Town Hall

Hadrian's Wall, a legacy of conquest

◆◆◆
HADRIAN'S WALL

Hadrian's Wall is one of the great 'musts' of the North. Perhaps the best tribute to the immensity of the Roman concept – a coast-to-coast wall for control and defence, 73 miles (117km) long, 15 feet (5m) high with a parapet on top, plus forts and communications links along the whole of its length – is the way much of it still survives, even though it has been used as a quarry for building stone since the Romans left in AD409. Defences began on the west coast. From **Bowness-on-Solway**, the wall ran eastwards past **Carlisle**, turf-on-earth in its early stages, almost all now gone, with the inland parts later refashioned in stone (reasonable chunks still visible), and then in solid stone for much of its remaining length, climbing along the crags of the **Whin Sill** in the centre of the country (here the wall is extremely well-preserved) and finally descending to **Newcastle** (now very fragmentary) and on to the coast. There was a large protective ditch in front of it. Behind lay a *vallum*, like the course of a sunken railway track, used for quick movement of men and supplies. Running through high, wide landscape, Hadrian's Wall is at its most dramatic from **Chollerford** to **Greenhead** and **Birdoswald**. The main museums and excavated sites are at **Chesters** (cavalry fort); the fort at **Housesteads**, right on the wall (a stiff walk uphill from the parking lot to a magnificent site); **Chesterholm**, well behind the wall (fort of *Vindolanda*, with personal belongings of Roman soldiers) and **Birdoswald** (recent excavations have revealed foundations of vast granaries and other buildings).

THE NORTH

Holy Island's 16th-century castle

♦♦
HOLY ISLAND AND THE NORTHUMBERLAND COAST

Low and romantic – except in summer when it is overcrowded – Holy Island, or Lindisfarne, lies just south of Berwick-upon-Tweed. It is reached by a causeway passable only at low tide. Tide tables posted at either end indicate when it is safe to cross. The monastery which was home to St Cuthbert, who evangelised the North, is long gone. The elegant ruins close to the village are those of the subsequent 11th-century priory.

Back on the mainland is the great bulk of **Bamburgh Castle**, one of a network built to keep out the Scots. It retains its fine keep and houses a museum of armour. The coast running south from here has **Seahouses** as its main tourist attraction. From here, boats are available to the Farne Islands, noted for seabirds and marine life.

♦♦♦
THE LAKE DISTRICT

It is up in the far northwest of England, in the Lake District, that the ruggedness of mountain and the sheen of water, the grey of stone and green of woods and pasture combine to form the most dramatic landscape in the country. The Lake District came into its own in the late 18th century as Wordsworth and the Romantics raised the banner of the sublimity of nature. Nowadays the Lake District can seem uncomfortably crowded in high summer. It may also be rainy. But even with the drawbacks, it would be a great shame to omit this small region – less than 40 miles (64km) across – from a tour of England.

The key to it all is variety, with no two mountains looking remotely similar: precipices alternating with rounded summits, high ridges leading down to boulder-strewn slopes, pastures running upwards, defined by grey stone walls, till suddenly they encounter impossible-seeming crags. The **Scafell Pikes**, at 3,205 feet (977m), occupy the highest ground. This cluster rises slightly to the west of centre, in company with the **Old Man of Coniston** and **Langdale Pikes**. Skiddaw, at 3,055 feet (931m), is the biggest in the north, while **Helvellyn**, kindly on one side, steep and ridged along the other, stands just to the north of centre. In and among them all there lie the Lakes, at least as varied in atmosphere as the mountains.

The Southern Lakes

Arriving by road from the southeast, on the M6 motorway, **Kendal**, home of Kendal mint-cake, is the first outpost of the Lake District. This attractive little stone-built town lies across the River Kent. Katherine Parr, sixth wife of Henry VIII, was born in the ruined castle on a grassy hill above the river to the east. The family had their own chapel in the five-aisled parish church. Close by is **Abbot's Hall**, a Georgian house open to the public, with a good local museum in the stables. Proceeding to the Lakes proper, the visitor soon arrives at the two side-by-side settlements of **Windermere** and **Bowness-in-Windermere**, together the effective capital of the Southern Lakes, on the banks of Lake Windermere.

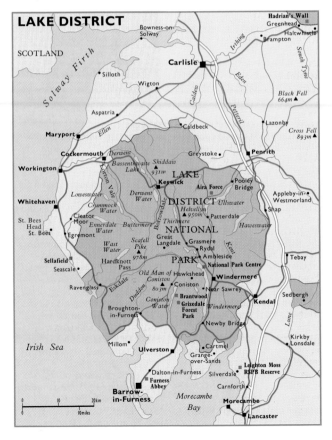

Both towns are pleasant enough but nothing more. Every second house appears to be a bed and breakfast establishment, a hotel or guest house. Windermere is the largest of the lakes and, beautiful as it is, by far the noisiest, with a good supply of ferries, powerboats and other craft.

Boats may be rented at Bowness.

Most excursions from Windermere involve passing through the traffic bottleneck at the top of the lake. Immediately to the north of this point are the town of **Ambleside** and the villages of **Grasmere** and **Rydal**, both very small. Grasmere in particular is wonderfully set among the hills. This, with a southwesterly extension to take in **Hawkshead** and **Esthwaite Water**, is Wordsworth country. Wordsworth was born in Cockermouth in the Northern Lakes (see opposite). He went to grammar school in Hawkshead, a tightly clustered little Lakeland village of lanes and small stone houses. His carved initials still survive on a school desk, as does Anne Tyson's cottage, where he stayed. Also in the village is a new **Beatrix Potter Museum**. After her marriage Beatrix Potter lived in a farmhouse at Near Sawrey, not far off, here producing many of her best-loved children's books. Pushing on briefly beyond Hawkshead, still in a southwesterly direction, one soon reaches **Coniston Water**, a lake with farmland fringes,

overshadowed to the north by the bulk of the Old Man of Coniston. Donald Campbell died here in 1967, attempting to break the world waterspeed record. Above the east shore stands **Brantwood**, home of John Ruskin, guide to 19th-century architectural taste and author of *The Stones of Venice*. Returning to Grasmere, one may pick up the Wordsworth trail with a visit to **Dove Cottage**, where he lived as a young man with his sister Dorothy and wrote many of his greatest works. Buried behind other buildings, with stone walls and an accompanying yew tree, flag floors and coal-burning grates downstairs, this modest dwelling is everybody's notion of an English cottage. Upstairs there is a small selection of Wordsworth's possessions. The **Wordsworth Museum** in

Grasmere Island: a summer retreat

an adjacent building is an outstanding portrayal of the whole Romantic movement and its connections with the Lake District.

Rydal Mount, the house of Wordsworth's later years, is half way between Grasmere and Ambleside, set high on a steep bank above Rydal Water. Like Ruskin's home, it is no mansion, but rather a very comfortable English home, with crooked floorboards and any quantity of Wordsworth furniture and fittings and family documents. The sloping garden, with the lawn giving way to shrubbery and shrubbery giving way to trees, is also a great pleasure.

William Wordsworth and Mary, his wife, are buried in Grasmere churchyard. Their gravestone may be found close by the stream.

The Northern Lakes
The accent here is more on lake and landscape, less on literature. **Keswick**, set close by much-praised **Derwent Water**, is the undisputed capital and, like Ambleside and Windermere, can be extremely crowded at Easter and in August. Outside these periods one may enjoy its lively streets and shops.
Crummock Water and **Ennerdale Water**, to the west, are among the least interfered-with of the Lakes, but **Bassenthwaite Lake**, to the north, suffers somewhat from the proximity of a double-lane highway leading to Cockermouth. (William Wordsworth was born here in a large and stately house, set back from the road behind iron railings.) **Ullswater**, to the east, must surely be the loveliest of the lakes, curving under Helvellyn at one end, tranquilly pastoral at the other. It is a favourite with windsurfers.
Up to the north here, almost out of the Lake District, is **Caldbeck**, a village with an interesting mill museum and, in its churchyard, the white-painted tombstone of John Peel, early-rising huntsman celebrated in song.
The best of the Lake District lies within the Lake District National Park. The park information centre is at **Brockhole**, between Windermere and Ambleside (tel: (09662) 6601).

THE NORTH

◆◆
NORTH YORK MOORS
North Yorkshire
This wild open moorland, intersected by green dales and conifer plantations, is bounded to the south by the Vale of Pickering, to the west by the Hambleton Hills; the Cleveland Hills make up the northern border and its eastern boundaries are the North Sea. In the summer the moors are purple with heather. Apart from the occasional isolated village this is empty country. This was not always so, as Bronze Age standing stones and earthworks testify. Medieval travellers erected stone crosses on these wild wastes as boundary stones and waymarkers – among them, **Ralph Cross** and **Fat Betty**. These are still orienteering aids. A modern landmark which has another function is the Early Warning System on **Fylingdales Moor**, a sinister composition of white orbs. Visitors often use small towns like **Pickering**, on the southern edge of the moors, or **Helmsley**, on the edge of the Cleveland Hills, as a base for exploration. Pickering is memorable as the terminus of the steam and diesel-driven **North Yorkshire Moors Railway** – a favourite method of entering the moors through Newtondale during the summer.

Helmsley is a lovely market town with grand houses and pale stone cottages and a large market square marked by an ancient cross. The remains of the 12th-century **castle** stand high amid earthworks just outside the centre. **Rievaulx Abbey** is within walking distance.

Meander through the North York Moors

Other popular moorland villages include **Hutton-le-Hole**, built round an old-fashioned green and down either side of a long stream. This is a good entry point to **Farndale**, where the chief attraction in springtime is the sight of hillsides covered in wild daffodils. For a reminder of a less idyllic aspect of moorland life, the village of **Rosedale Abbey** has interesting remains of ironstone mines.

This is pre-eminently walking country. The **Cleveland Way** is a route of about 100 miles (160km), from Helmsley northwards in a semicircle to the east coast and then back down to Scarborough. Less ambitious strollers may settle for the **Lyke Wake Walk**, 40 miles (64km) across the centre of the moors from Osmotherly to Ravenscar.

The **Danby Lodge National Park Centre** at the head of the Esk Valley is a good source of information at Lodge Lane, Danby (tel: (0287) 660654).

◆
RICHMOND
North Yorkshire
This small town built high on the banks of the River Swale gave its name to the palace of Richmond, in west London. It was one of the earliest Norman fortifications, built in 1071 and occupying a strategic position high above the river. Now, it is another romantic Yorkshire ruin with the town draped round its shoulders.

The main focus of Richmond is the large cobbled market place, complete with a market cross, from 1771, and a large number of well preserved 18th-century houses. A theatre built in 1788 has been restored to its original looks and function. Luckily, the main road carries passing traffic around the periphery of the town. One of the great pleasures of Richmond is strolling its streets or making a circuit of the castle walls or walking by the river. A riverside walk takes you to the ruined 12th-century **Easby Abbey**.

◆
WHITBY
North Yorkshire
Though past its days of glory as an important whaling and ship-building centre, Whitby is a lively fishing port and resort on the North Yorkshire coast. It straddles the Esk estuary; to the east lies the older part of town and the fishermen's quarter, which has strong associations with the explorer Captain Cook. The house where he served his apprenticeship in Grape Lane is now the **Captain Cook Memorial Museum**.

From the north end of the main street 199 stone steps lead to **St Mary's Church**. The plain 12th-century exterior gives no hint of the decorated and galleried interior of the 17th and 18th centuries. Bram Stoker, 19th-century author of *Dracula*, has his long-toothed hero taking refuge in this very churchyard after a storm. On the cliffs above the church stand the dramatic ruins of

Whitby Abbey, founded in 657 by the redoubtable St Hilda as a mixed community of nuns and monks. It rapidly became a religious centre of some importance; the famous Synod of Whitby was convened here in 664 to integrate ecclesiastical practice between the Celtic and Roman traditions. It was attacked by the Danes but re-established by Benedictine monks in 1078. The modern part of Whitby lies on the west side of the estuary. Here is the whalebone arch, Captain Cook's statue, most of the Victorian town (Whitby produced much of the jet used in Victorian jewellery) and the modern coastal resort. To the north of Whitby, **Staithes** is a pretty little fishing village at the bottom of a cliff so steep that visitors are advised to leave their cars and walk down. It lost its position as an important fishing port when the harbour proved too small for modern trawlers. Captain Cook spent some time here as a young man before he left for Whitby *en route* to Tahiti, New Zealand and Australia. Other resorts on the Yorkshire coast include **Robin Hood's Bay**, with its 3-mile (5km) stretch of beach, and tiny cobbled streets, very crowded in summer; and **Scarborough**, with two sandy bays and a Norman castle on a headland. The 'Queen of the Yorkshire Coast' has been a seaside resort since the 18th century and looks set to continue indefinitely, despite local complaints that it has become too commercialised.

◆◆◆
YORK
North Yorkshire
Eboracum to the Romans and *Jorvik* to the Vikings, York has always been the unofficial capital of the North and the second city of the realm. It is also one of the most beautiful, surrounded by nearly 3 miles (5km) of substantial medieval walls entered through the original gates, or bars, as they are known here. The best way for a visitor to see the walls is to walk along them – also a favourite pastime of locals on a sunny Sunday afternoon. They were built in the 13th century on earth ramparts constructed by the Danes and enlarged by the Normans – both of whom had the advantage of what remained of the original Roman structure. The section of the wall around the Minster is the most dramatic and lovely, with views of the old medieval town and the gardens surrounding the Treasurer's House and Deanery.

York has its own archbishop. As befits the second episcopal see after Canterbury, the great architectural star of the city is undoubtedly the **Minster**. The largest Gothic cathedral north of the Alps, built in creamy gold stone in a mixture of every Gothic style from the 13th to 15th centuries, it dominates the northern corner of the city. The stained glass, executed by local craftsmen, is a notable feature; apart from its quality and variety, it represents the greatest quantity of medieval glass in any single English building, a total of 126 windows. The grisaille lancet windows in the north transept, known as the Five Sisters, are particularly fine. The chapter house is an example of late 13th-century architectural engineering – its vaulted wooden ceiling, spanning 64 feet (19m), is unsupported by any central column.

The medieval area around the Minster contains much of York's best preserved architecture, some awesome and grand, some of more domestic proportions. **The Shambles** is probably the most famous of these medieval streets, originally Fleshammels – the street of butchers, but now offering more varied stock. **Newgate Market**, near by, has been trading daily for centuries.

York has many museums, and the **Jorvik Viking Centre** in Coppergate is undoubtedly the most popular. Sit in a time car and be transported through the history of York to the Viking age, where models, sound effects and even smells bring to life the Viking village which was excavated on this site by the York Archaeological Trust. If the waxworks and stereo sound of Jorvik make you eager to learn more, walk along to the **ARC** – Archaeological Resource Centre – in St Saviourgate. **Castle Museum**, off Tower Street, used to be a women's prison but now houses a huge collection of exhibits on the social history of York. They include shop-lined streets, the Coppergate Helmet, made for

The beautiful Minster at York

an Anglo-Saxon warrior in the 8th century and rediscovered by two archaeological workers on the Jorvik site, and the condemned cell where Dick Turpin, the highwayman, was held.

The **Yorkshire Museum**, in Museum Gardens, has displays of Roman, Viking and Anglo-Saxon treasures.

The **Museum of Automata** in Tower Street is charming and instructive. At the touch of a button a punk hammers a nail into his head, women leap up waving burning bras; the exhibits are clever and witty and some make a serious social comment.

Other museums of note include the **National Railway Museum** in Leeman Road, the **City Art Gallery** in Exhibition Square and **The York Story Heritage Centre** on Castlegate.

Accommodation
Askrigg
The **King's Arms**, Market Place (tel: (0969) 50258) has comfortable, modernised bedrooms furnished in period style.

Durham
The **Royal County**, in Old Elvet (tel: (091) 386 6821) has been refurbished to a very high standard and has a variety of restaurants. The **Three Tuns** in New Elvet (tel: (091) 386 4326) retains some of its original coaching inn features.

Lake District
Monoleys Hotel and Restaurant (tel: (06998) 234 & 367) is situated in the centre of **Caldbeck**. Bedrooms are well furnished and a very good standard of cooking is provided. The newly built **Riverside Hotel**, Stramongate Bridge, **Kendal** (tel: (0539) 724707), has spacious rooms, all *en suite*. The **Chaucer House Hotel**, Ambleside Road, **Keswick** (tel: (07687) 72318) is a friendly, comfortable hotel.

York
The **Viking Hotel** in North Street (tel: (0904) 659822) has a choice of three restaurants and caters well to business people. Close to the city centre, the **Grange Hotel**, Clifton (tel: (0904) 644744) has well-equipped bedrooms, and the Ivy Restaurant serves French and English country cooking. **Heworth Court**, 76–78 Heworth Green (tel: (0904) 425156) is a comfortable hotel with a cosy restaurant.

THE SOUTH

The South is the part of England which was earliest settled and always the most populated. In the eyes of others in Britain it is the soft underbelly of the country – where the politics are conservative and the living is easy. The South means easy access to the continent from a coastline of old resorts, choked roads skirting round the salubrious suburbs of Surrey and Kent, the green stock-broker belts of Sussex and Hampshire.

The topography is simple. Along most of the length of the coast, there rises a high rolling ridge of downland – the **South Downs** – grass on chalk extending from beyond

Winchester in the west to Eastbourne in the east. Here it reaches right down to the sea, producing such memorable vertical falls of chalk as **Beachy Head** and the seven promontories of the **Seven Sisters**. Behind this first barrier of downs, the land flattens somewhat to form the rolling farmlands of the **Weald** and the orchards and hop fields of **Kent**. Only **Ashdown Forest** in Sussex remains as a reminder that this area was once entirely forested. From here, the land rises again suddenly, in another chalky barrier. This constitutes the **North Downs**, which lie in a long ridge blocking immediate access to London and the Thames valley. The North Downs extend from Guildford in the

west towards the coast at Rochester, then curve down to form the white cliffs of Dover in the east. Here, the land plunges to the sea in tremendous sheer cliffs.

The South, from the coast to London, has been a virtual land corridor for every invader and settler over the centuries. The Celts, Romans, Saxons and Danes all helped to tread a highway through these counties, followed (in the last successful invasion) by the Normans in 1066. The South Coast bristles with fortresses. **Dover Castle** is a good example of the continuous use of fortifications through the centuries right up to World War II. The round martello towers which still stand guard on the coastline between

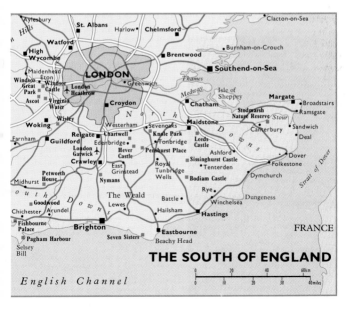

THE SOUTH OF ENGLAND

Hastings and Eastbourne (built against Napoleon) are a reminder of the constant fear of a European invasion.

The great shipyards at **Portsmouth** and **Chatham** are now only memorials of their former glory under Henry VII and Henry VIII. The historic dockyard has been preserved at Chatham; at Portsmouth, *The Victory*, Lord Nelson's flagship, is on view to the public together with the remains of the Tudor warship, the *Mary Rose*, recently raised from the mud which had protected her ever since she foundered in the 16th century. This is one of the parts of Britain most thronged with castles – **Bodiam**, **Leeds** and **Arundel** and – most floral, with scores of gardens – **Wisley**,

Nelson died on The Victory

Sissinghurst and **Nymans**. It is also splendid with great houses – **Petworth** and **Penshurst** and **Broadlands** (home of the late Lord Mountbatten).

WHAT TO SEE

◆

ARUNDEL

West Sussex

The great towered castle dominates the town of Arundel, built at its feet and tumbling down the steep hill to the River Arun below. The castle is the seat of the Duke of Norfolk, the leading Catholic peer of the realm. It had its origins in the 11th century, but most of what the visitor now sees is the work of 18th- and 19th-century restorers. The state apartments, with a fine collection of furniture and portraits, have been entirely rebuilt – but grandly.

In the town, the 14th-century parish church of **St Nicholas** has some interesting wall paintings. Behind the altar, the lovely Fitzalan Chapel has been divided from the rest of the church by an iron grill and is the private property of the Duke of Norfolk. The imposing Catholic cathedral of **St Philip Neri**, built in the second half of the 19th century by the incumbent duke, was dedicated to a 16th-century ancestor. He died in the Tower of London, accused of offering prayers for the success of the Spanish Armada.

About 10 miles (16km) north of Arundel lies **Petworth House**, built in the latter years of the 17th century in the grounds of a great park designed by Capability Brown. The house is worth visiting, not least for its splendid collection of paintings, including work by Van Dyck, Titian, Gainsborough, Reynolds and Turner.

◆
BATTLE
East Sussex
It was here that the outcome of a battle in 1066 changed the shape of English history. The fields on the slopes near this small town, six miles (9km) north of Hastings, saw the defeat of the Saxon king Harold at the hands of William, Duke of Normandy. To commemorate his victory, William built an **abbey** on the spot where Harold raised his standard. Much of the abbey was destroyed in the Dissolution of the Monasteries in the second half of the 16th century. The fine gatehouse still stands and the Abbot's house is now an independent school. Continuing eastwards along the coast, **Winchelsea** (a 13th-century town now shrunk into a picturesque village) and ancient **Rye** are both rewarding brief stops. Rye, the bigger of the two, is built on the steep sides of a hill with narrow cobbled streets. The church of **St Mary's**, grand with flying buttresses, sits on top of the hill, tightly pressed all around by ancient houses in a cosy square. Its 16th-century clock is said to be the oldest in England. At one corner of the square stands **Ypres Tower**,

the remains of a 13th-century fort.

BRIGHTON
East Sussex
A one-time fishing village turned seaside spa, Brighton shot into the big time in 1786 when the Prince Regent (later George IV) came here to live with his mistress, Maria Fitzherbert. Now it is a crowded and lively town with a young population.
The **Royal Pavilion**, a stone's throw from the sea front, was built for the Prince Regent in 1815. The visitor is hit squarely between the eyes by this confection, a mixture of every style, real or imagined, that anyone has ever associated with the Orient. Inside, the style favours Chinese with a touch of ancient Egypt and a smidgeon of 'Hindoo'. The banqueting room, to give just one example, has a high domed ceiling decorated with the giant leaves of a plantain tree and lotus flower lights suspended from a winged dragon.
Round the corner in Church Street, the **Brighton Museum and Art Gallery** has a collection of 19th- and 20th-century art, and an exhibition of Sussex archaeology. **The Lanes** in the centre of Brighton are the oldest part of the town, narrow little streets, formerly of fishermen's cottages, now of shops and boutiques. The sea front at Brighton extends for miles with a busy marina some way to the east.

Canterbury Cathedral

◆◆◆
CANTERBURY
Kent

The modern city with a medieval heart, on the banks of the River Stour, is as much a place of pilgrimage today as it has always been. In the 6th century, Canterbury was the capital of the Saxon king Ethelbert, who converted to Christianity in 597. From that time, Canterbury has been the seat of the Archbishop, the Primate of all England, and the country's spiritual centre. Pilgrimages began in earnest after the murder in the cathedral of Archbishop Thomas à Becket in 1170. He had first been appointed chancellor by Henry II and then Archbishop of Canterbury. The king fondly imagined that his servant would remain loyal to him in the conflict of interest then

raging between the church and state. Instead, Becket proved himself a devout and committed son of the church, determined to resist the king. Henry's famous cry of 'Who will rid me of this troublesome priest?' led to his murder by four of the king's knights while he was saying vespers in his own cathedral. The ensuing outcry induced the king himself to come here to do penance.

Canterbury then became a shrine of great sanctity and power. Chaucer's *Canterbury Tales* describes a band of pilgrims who came from Southwark in London, but there were pilgrims from all over the country and from Europe too. Approach the cathedral as the early pilgrims did, by the High Street and through narrow

Mercery Lane. Bottles of holy water and pilgrim badges and remembrances of the saint are no longer hawked about in this street but the town still makes a good living out of the martyrdom. The lane leads into **Butter Market**, a tiny square with a war memorial in its centre. Past **Christ Church Gate**, substantial and decorated with coats of arms, there stands the great Gothic **cathedral**, built of stone from the quarries of Caen in France. A stone slab in the northwest transept marks the site of the murder. The shrine to the martyr in Trinity Chapel was destroyed by Henry VIII, but a candle still burns in his memory. Notice the depression in the stone steps leading up to the chapel and the area where the shrine once stood – worn down by the knees of centuries of pilgrims. Henry IV and Edward the Black Prince are buried here. Adjacent to the cathedral stand the remains of a former 7th-century monastery, now **King's School**, a public (that is to say, private) boys' school endowed by Henry VIII. The Elizabethan playwright Christopher Marlowe was a pupil and so, unhappily for him, was the novelist W Somerset Maugham. Bomb damage from World War II destroyed much of the city but there is a lot left to see. Important monuments include the remains of **St Augustine's Abbey**, founded by Augustine in 597; **St Thomas's Hospital**, where poor pilgrims from the 12th century could rest and recover after their journeys; the **Poor Priests' Hospital**, now housing the **Canterbury Heritage Exhibition**; **St Martin's Church**, probably the oldest church in the country; and the **Weavers' Houses**, half-timbered houses occupied by refugee Huguenot weavers in the 16th and 17th centuries. Parts of the old city walls still stand but of the original gates, only **West Gate** remains, now housing a museum (temporarily closed). The coast around Canterbury is littered with rather old-fashioned resorts. **Sandwich**, though no longer strictly on the coast, is definitely worth a visit.

◆
CHICHESTER
West Sussex

This market town, situated between the South Downs and the sea, was founded by the Romans. The best of the architecture is of the 18th century, when the town became prosperous as a trading port; the **Pallant**, a Georgian precinct, is the best example. The Norman **cathedral**, begun in 1091, is famous for its 15th-century detached bell tower (the only one in England), as well as for its brilliant 20th-century altar tapestry by John Piper, paintings by Graham Sutherland and stained-glass windows by Marc Chagall. There is an outstanding **Market Cross** dating from 1501. Sir Laurence Olivier began an annual summer theatre festival here which attracts a devoted following.

Near by, to the southwest of Chichester, lies **Fishbourne Palace,** featuring the remains of the north wing of a huge 1st-century Roman mansion, once occupied by a British chieftain. It was excavated in the 1960s and there are wonderfully intact mosaic floors and underfloor heating systems.

♦
DOVER
Kent
This town with its harbour, docks, hovercraft, jetfoil, and now the site of the English terminus for the new Channel Tunnel, is mostly occupied with cross-Channel traffic. Not surprising, as the Straits of Dover, 17 miles (27km) across, offer the shortest sea route to Europe. Dover is the chief of the Cinque Ports. Since the Norman conquest it has managed to discharge that responsibility with some flair, despite being sacked by the French in the 13th century and heavily bombed by the Germans in the 20th. Fine buildings still survive, most of them on the north side of the Market Square. They include the Roman **Painted House,** with interesting murals and a Roman central heating system. The **Town Hall** incorporates the 14th-century Maison Dieu Hall, once a pilgrim's hostel. The attractions of the town pale beside those of **Dover Castle,** above the town. No ruin this, being in constant use as a refuge and place of security. The keep, 21 feet (6m) thick, was built by Henry II at the end of the 12th century against

the French.
As always, the Romans were here first. They left an ancient *pharos,* or lighthouse. The Saxons who followed used old Roman bricks to build the church of **St Mary de Castro** beside it – too tidily restored for modern taste. Above all, it is the view across the Channel and along the coast which has given these Dover cliffs a special place in the history of the island.

♦
ISLE OF WIGHT
This small island, 12 miles (19km) long 21 miles (34km) wide, lies off the Hampshire coast and enjoys its own independent administrative status.
Much of the island is wooded and hilly (large areas are protected by the National Trust) with some spectacular cliff scenery. It is probably most famous for the sailing regatta which takes place every year from the harbour at Cowes. It received its royal imprimatur from the Prince Regent, a tie further strengthened by the patronage of Queen Victoria, who spent her summers here. **Osborne House,** where she lived, a little inland from Cowes, has been left as a perfect example of high Victorian domestic architecture and furnishings. The popularity of the wide sandy beaches make the island very crowded in the summer. There are frequent ferry and hydrofoil services from Southampton and Portsmouth.

◆◆
NEW FOREST
Hampshire

So-called by William the Conqueror, this huge area (93,000 acres/37,600 hectares) in the southwest corner of Hampshire has historically been a protected royal hunting ground. From the 16th century, its forests were used as a source of timber and today, too, there are new forestry plantations. Even so, it retains the largest area of native deciduous forest – beech, oak and holly – in the country. Thanks to the unfertile heathland surrounding these forests there has never been much demand for cultivation and the great stretches of open heathland, marsh and bog harbour much wildlife. Wild ponies roam freely about the forest, occasionally bringing the traffic to a standstill as they cross the roads that intersect the forest. **Lyndhurst** is a popular base for exploring the New Forest. Visitors might care to stop at **Stoney Cross**, site of the Rufus Stone, where William Rufus, son of the conqueror, was killed by an arrow in 1100, in what purported to be a hunting accident.

Those more taken with stately homes and vintage cars should go to **Beaulieu** (pronounced Bewley), where they will find **Palace House**, stately home of Lord Montagu; here is the **National Motor Museum**, with a remarkable collection of veteran and vintage cars and motorcycles and the ruins of **Beaulieu Abbey**, once a grand Cistercian house founded by King John in 1204.

Morris (folk) dancers

◆
TUNBRIDGE WELLS
Kent

Royal Tunbridge Wells is the full name of this Kentish spa town; it had enjoyed royal patronage for centuries before the lofty distinction of 'royal' was given to it by Edward VII in 1909. Its health-giving chalybeate water was discovered by Lord North in 1606 and instantly became popular in court circles.

The **Pantiles**, a wide, colonnaded promenade lined with balustraded houses and leading to a major source of the spa water, were built in 1638, at the time of Tunbridge's maximum popularity. The name Pantiles is taken from the original square clay tiles which paved this area. Sadly, none of them remain; the last few are in the care of the British Museum.

THE SOUTH

The town's position on the Kent-Sussex border makes it a good base for many other places of interest. One excellent excursion might be a little northwards to **Knole Park**, in Sevenoaks. Built in the latter years of the 15th century, the house was given to Thomas Sackville by his cousin Queen Elizabeth I in 1566. The most famous member of the family in modern times was Vita Sackville-West, the subject of Virginia Woolf's novel *Orlando*.

Sissinghurst Castle also has memories of Vita Sackville-West. The famous gardens here were entirely created by her and her husband Sir Harold Nicolson in the 1930s. Her White Garden is the most admired – only flowers and plants of silver, grey and white.

Chartwell, near Westerham, is the house bought by Sir Winston Churchill as a family home in 1922. The original building is a 14th-century farmhouse and far from grand. The house may be visited – Churchill's own rooms remain largely as he left them – as well as the garden studio where he painted, and the brick wall which he constructed in the garden.

Hever Castle, near Edenbridge, was the childhood home of Anne Boleyn; Henry VIII courted her here. The house was bought by the American millionaire, William Waldorf Astor, later Lord Astor, in 1903, and completely renovated, restored and extended.

◆◆
WINCHESTER
Hampshire

The statue of King Alfred with drawn sword stands at the end of the Broadway – a fitting symbol for the capital of the early kingdom of Wessex and, with London, joint capital of England after the Norman conquest. It has remained an important city throughout history. Recent rebuilding and excavation work have thrown up hitherto hidden Iron Age defences, a Saxon church and a Roman forum to add to the wealth of medieval, Tudor and 18th-century building that already exists in Winchester. The historical focus of the town is the **cathedral**. Compared to other cathedrals, it may lack loftiness but the Perpendicular style nave, built on the site of an early Roman forum, is very large, and said to be the longest of its kind in Europe. It houses the remains of such notables as King Cnut (Canute), William Rufus, Jane Austen (the house where she died is in Winchester) and Izaak Walton, author of the *Compleat Angler*, as well as the bones of St Swithun. According to one version of the story, St Swithun had expressed a wish to be buried in the churchyard. In defiance of this, his remains were moved in to the body of the church on 15 July 971. Immediately following this act of disobedience, the rain poured down on the town for 40 days, non-stop. The legend now warns that if it rains on 15 July, it will continue to pour

down for 40 days.
The cathedral also houses rare books and manuscripts and the spectacularly illuminated 12th-century Winchester Bible, which is kept in the South Transept Library.
Winchester is also notable for its public school, **Winchester College**, one of the most prestigious in England, reached through King's Gate, south of the cathedral. It was founded in 1382 by William of Wykeham to provide an education for 70 poor scholars and prepare them for a career in the church. The modern college is an interesting combination of medieval and Victorian buildings. The chapel, the war memorial cloister, the old cloisters and chantry are open to the public. Southwards from the college, the 12th-century **Hospital of St Cross** maintains its tradition of hospitality to travellers and pilgrims. The modern traveller may call and ask for the traditional Wayfarer's Dole and receive a sip of ale and a piece of bread.

◆◆◆
WINDSOR CASTLE
Berkshire
The towers and walls of this largest inhabited castle in the world can be seen rising above the Thames for miles around. It has been continously in use since William the Conqueror. When the Queen is in residence at the castle the royal flag flies from the Round Tower and the state apartments are closed to the public.

St George's Chapel, on the right as you enter the castle, is a lovely late Perpendicular building. Henry VIII and Charles I were among those buried here and there is a memorial chapel to the Queen's father, George VI.
Queen Mary's Dolls' House is one of the most popular sights at Windsor. It was designed by Sir Edwin Lutyens, a leading architect, to raise money for a children's charity. An exhibition of toys belonging to the Queen and Princess Margaret is shown in glass cases.
As at Buckingham Palace, the changing of the guard at Windsor takes place every day in the summer and every other day in the winter.

Windsor Castle

THE SOUTH

Accommodation
Brighton
St Catherine's Lodge,
Kingsway (tel: (0273) 778181) is
a well-established seafront
hotel with fine Regency
features. Close to the seafront
and town, **Courtlands**, 19–27
The Drive (tel: (0273) 731055)
has a nicely appointed
restaurant. The **Whitehaven**,
34 Wilbury Road
(tel: (0273) 778355) offers well
equipped modern
accommodation and a fine
restaurant.

Canterbury
The **Chaucer** in Ivy Lane
(tel: (0227) 464427) has compact
bedrooms, though larger
rooms are available. The
Falstaff is a modernised 16th-
century coaching inn in St
Dunstan's Street
(tel: (0227) 462138) with a
traditional restaurant. The
Canterbury, 71 New Dover
Road (tel: (0227) 450551) is a
pleasant Georgian-style hotel
with a very friendly atmosphere.

Isle of Wight
Most of the rooms in **The
Albion Hotel** in Freshwater
(tel: (0983) 753631) have a
balcony or terrace facing the
sea. Good standards of
cooking. The **Biskra House
Beach Hotel**, 17 St Thomas's
Street, Ryde (tel: (0983) 67913)
has been thoughtfully
furnished and well equipped.
The **Melville Hall Hotel**,
Melville Street, Sandown
(tel: (0983) 406526) is close to
all local amenities. It offers
modern bedrooms, lounge,
coffee shop, snack bar,
restaurant and bar.

Winchester
The Royal Hotel, St Peter
Street (tel: (0962) 840840) has
en suite facilities in all rooms.
There is an attractive
conservatory-style restaurant.
A purpose-built hotel, the
Winchester Moat House,
Worthy Lane (tel: (0962) 68102)
offers well-equipped
bedrooms and a restaurant
featuring set menus. The
Wessex Hotel, Paternoster
Row (tel: (0962) 61611) has a
selection of accommodation of
different standards.

Restaurants
Brighton
The **Eaton Garden** is
conveniently situated in the
commercial centre of Hove
(tel: (0273) 738921) and offers
an enjoyable range of English
and Continental dishes. **Le
Grandgousier**, 15 Western
Street (tel: (0273) 772005) is a
small but well established
French restaurant. The six-
course fixed price menu is
especially good value for the
money.

Canterbury
Michael's Restaurant at 74
Wincheap (tel: (0227) 767411)
offers interesting and
imaginative dishes and both *à
la carte* and set-price menus.
Ristorante Tuo e Mio, 16 The
Borough (tel: (0227) 761471) has
a fine Italian menu which
includes excellent seafood
specialities.

Isle of Wight
Sullivan's, 10 Bath Road,
Cowes (tel: (0983) 297021) has a
short menu which features new
style and classical dishes.

THE SOUTHWEST

The West Country: these words are full of promise, suggesting beach and cliff, afternoon teas and old-fashioned seaside vacations. In fact the West Country is a little larger than just the westernmost peninsula of Devon and Cornwall. The real West Country is defined by a particular speech pattern, made up of rolling 'r's with broad, soft vowels, which can be heard in Bath and Bristol and everywhere west of a curving line that runs down through the Wiltshire towns of Marlborough and Salisbury to meet the coast in Dorset, by Poole and Bournemouth. Everything west of here is West Country proper.

Thomas Hardy's home

The West Country is extraordinarily rich in prehistoric sites; **Stonehenge** and its neighbours are among the greatest early monuments of all Europe. Along with Wales, the West Country harboured the last of the Celts as they retreated in the face of Saxon, Danish, then Norman invasion. It is here, above all, that legends of King Arthur, mysterious British chieftain and romantic hero, have their beginnings. Later, it was the western peninsula which launched Britain's explorers and pirates and defeated the proud Spanish Armada. Two more modern invaders landed here: the Duke of Monmouth in 1685, in a doomed attempt to seize the British crown, and, three years later, the Dutch William of Orange, who was entirely successful in the same objective.

With the exception of Bristol and Swindon and, surprisingly enough, some parts of distant Cornwall, the West Country is little industrialised. Wiltshire and Dorset are chalk landscapes with downs, broken by one or two stretches of heath and upland – **Salisbury Plain**, nowadays dominated in parts by the military, and **Egdon Heath**, as described by the novelist Thomas Hardy. It is Hardy's spirit above all, replete with a sense of rural tragedy, which broods over Dorset.

Wiltshire is an inland county; the best part of the Dorset coast is a mixture of cliff and cove, with at least two towns of great charm – **Weymouth** and **Lyme Regis**. Lyme Regis features in Jane Austen's novel *Persuasion* and was the scene

THE SOUTHWEST

for the book and film of *The French Lieutenant's Woman* by John Fowles.

Bristol is the major city of the west, possibly worth a visit as an adjunct to Bath, but not a must. Its most spectacular sight is a lofty bridge over a gorge – built by the great railway engineer Isambard Kingdom Brunel. What is most remarkable about Bristol, however, is its history. Right up to modern times, it has always been a major port, working the ocean routes between Europe, Africa and America and rising to wealth as a slavers' city. Moving on southwestwards, rural Somerset comes next, a place of considerable beauty, with several low ranges of hills, notably the **Mendips** and **Quantocks** and ending with the bleaker wilds of **Exmoor**. Close by Bristol, the country is

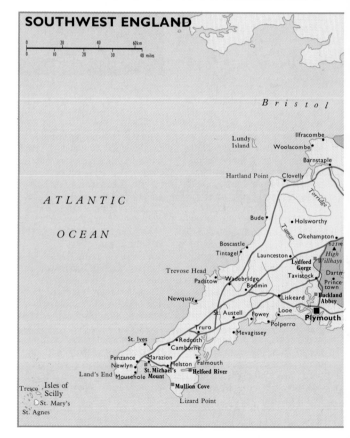

SOUTHWEST ENGLAND

0   20   40   60km
0 10 20 30 40 miles

B r i s t o l

ATLANTIC

OCEAN

Lundy Island
Ilfracombe
Woolacombe
Barnstaple
Hartland Point
Clovelly
Bude
Holsworthy
Boscastle
Tintagel
Okehampton
621m
High Willhays
Trevose Head
Launceston
Lydford Gorge
Tavistock
Dartm
Padstow
Wadebridge
Prince- town
Newquay
Bodmin
Buckland Abbey
Liskeard
St. Austell
Fowey
Looe
Plymouth
Truro
Polperro
Mevagissey
St. Ives
Redruth
Camborne
Penzance
Marazion
Newlyn
Helston
Falmouth
Land's End
St. Michael's Mount
Mousehole
Helford River
Tresco
Isles of Scilly
Mullion Cove
St. Mary's
Lizard Point
St. Agnes
Torridge
Tamar

green and moist, marked by the tall towers of 'wool' churches, for this was one of many parts of England which achieved early wealth through sheep. The mysterious settlement of **Glastonbury**, once an island in a lake, and the delightful cathedral town of **Wells** are in this area. Exmoor is entirely different in mood. **Jamaica Inn**, which gave its name to a Daphne du Maurier novel, still plies its trade up in the middle of the moor.

The north coast faces the Atlantic and it is splendid, with high-rearing cliffs and sandy beaches. Craggy **Hartland Point**, awesome in a gale, looks out towards the Isle of Lundy at the mouth of the Bristol Channel. Tucked down not far away is the famous Devon beauty spot of **Clovelly**, a precipitous little village for

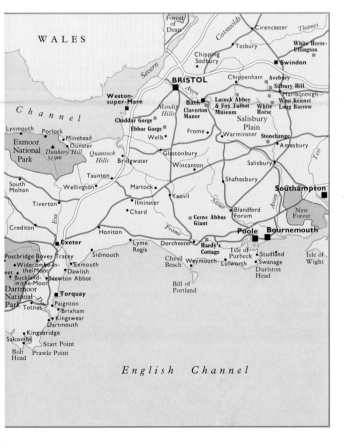

walkers only. Around lie holiday towns such as **Ilfracombe** and **Woolacombe**, with more of the same down into Cornwall. Here the cliffs and coves are equally impressive, with some marvellous little coastal spots for those prepared to walk. The south coast is equally interesting and perhaps more varied. Starting to the west of the cathedral city of **Exeter**, it includes the 'English Riviera' round **Torquay** and **Paignton**, known cumulatively as **Torbay**. Beyond the River Dart and **Dartmouth**, there comes an exceptionally lovely coastal pocket called the **Hams**, centred on **Kingsbridge** and the sailing resort of **Salcombe**. Here the inland parts at least are totally unspoilt. Inland again, there lurks the sterner country of **Dartmoor**.

Just along the south coast now is **Plymouth**, Britain's chief repository of maritime history. This was Drake's port when he defeated the Spanish Armada, and the Pilgrim Fathers of the Mayflower finally set off from here. Cornwall's south coast, which starts a leap out of Plymouth across the River Tamar, is full of picturesque small towns and tiny harbours: **Looe**, **Polperro**, **Fowey**, **Mevagissey** and the beauty-spots of the **Lizard** peninsula, England's southernmost point. At the end of it all, on the toe of Cornwall, there is more riviera – **Penzance** to the south, **St Ives**, an artists' colony, to the north. **Land's End** is right at the tip of the toe, now a major tourist spot.

WHAT TO SEE

BATH
Avon
Bath has been a World Heritage Site since 1987. Built in the valley of the River Avon, it climbs the surrounding hills in terraces of well preserved 18th-century elegance. It all began when the Romans built a temple over a hot spring that gushed out of the earth. They called it *Aquae Sulis*, invoking the Celtic deity Sulis and the Roman goddess of health, Minerva.

After the Romans left, the town, along with much else in Britain, fell into decay and disarray. The waters, though, were still in use – much favoured for the cure of skin ailments as well, in due course, as a remedy for syphilis. Bath's fortunes turned at the beginning of the 18th century, with the arrival of Beau Nash, grand arbiter of style who insisted on a general raising of tone among those taking the waters. John Wood and his son were soon engaged in transforming the architecture of Bath into the elegant row houses, the noble crescents and the grand circuses (circles) we see today. Fashionable and aspiring society flocked here. This no doubt contributed to the atmosphere of ossified gentility that Jane Austen found so tiresome. The city still emanates a faint air of bourgeois uprightness, tempered by a lively young population and a summer Arts Festival.

The **Roman Baths** are the town's premier attraction. Before you take a tour it is worth walking through the adjacent **museum**. The Romans used the Baths, essentially, as a gentlemen's health and social club. There was a comprehensive system of hot underfloor heating, warm baths and cold pools, complete with entertainments and opportunities to gossip and intrigue. The spring still bubbles, steaming away at a constant and tempting, 112°F (46.5°C). But you are not allowed even to dip a toe. There have been plans to put the waters to modern recreational use but they remain on the drawing board. At the end of the tour you can visit the high, chandeliered **Pump Room**. Here you can drink a glass of the spa waters as a musical trio plays.
Bath prides itself on the knowledge and enthusiasm of the guides who conduct free walking tours of the city. Their itinerary takes in the main Georgian architectural features such as the **Circus** and the **Royal Crescent**, an unbroken, unified row of 30 houses. Two in the middle comprise the luxurious **Royal Crescent Hotel**. **No 1 Royal Crescent** is a house preserved in 18th-century style. The **Assembly Rooms** near by, once the main social gathering point, are now an excellent **Costume Museum**.
The **abbey**, begun in the last year of the 15th century, is worth a visit.
Lacock Abbey and village lie

Bath Abbey from the Roman Baths

14 miles (22km) southeast of Bath. The abbey, founded in 1232, has remained in the hands of the Talbot family, since the Dissolution of the Monasteries in the 16th century. As well as the abbey, the Talbots owned the entire village of Lacock. Both have passed into the care of the National Trust and are preserved as far as possible in their original state: beautiful, though slightly 'pickled in aspic' (as the British would say). The Fox Talbot family, famous in the history of photography, continue to live in the abbey. The **Fox Talbot Museum of Early Photography** stands at the abbey gates.

◆◆
DARTMOOR
Devon

Often wracked by mist and rain, grazed by shaggy ponies and even shaggier Highland cattle, Dartmoor is a byword for ruggedness, all the more surprising because of its location in the generally gentle southwest. If walking, take a good map and wet weather gear and watch for the bright green of bogs among the darker heather. On a fine day, Dartmoor is an exhilarating place, with stretches of undulating moorland giving way to sizeable hills called 'tors', the same name used for the towers of granite that surmount them, stone piled on weathered stone in strange shapes, left behind by the Ice Age when surrounding earth was scraped away.

Dartmoor is specially rich in prehistoric sites, with stone circles incorporating boulders borrowed from the tors.

Medieval inhabitants mined for tin and bridged the rivers with long slabs of stone perched on casual-seeming stone-piled pillars. Several of these 'clapper bridges' still survive, the best at **Postbridge**. At **Dartmeet**, where only two spans out of the clapper bridge's four are left, the two branches of the Dart meet around the garden of an isolated house.

There are a number of pretty villages, among them **Buckland-in-the-Moor** and **Widecombe-in-the-Moor** – the latter celebrated in the song 'As I was going to Widdecombe Fair'. It was on Dartmoor that Sherlock Holmes dealt with the frightening matter of the Baskerville Hounds. At **Princetown**, high on the moor, there is a gaunt and depressing prison, built for prisoners during the Napoleonic Wars.

The whole of the Moor is included in the **Dartmoor National Park**.

The clapper bridge at Postbridge

◆
DARTMOUTH
Devon

This town, as its name suggests, is built close in to the mouth of the Dart, which is itself protected by a castle. It is a place of boats, ringing with seagulls, with the pink brick and white stone mass of the Royal Naval officers' college rearing above. For visitors, the greatest interest of Dartmouth may be the fact that the Pilgrim Fathers actually set out from here: English pilgrims in the *Mayflower* and Dutch (from Leiden) in the accident-prone *Speedwell*. They sailed on 7 September 1620, but the unseaworthiness of the *Speedwell* compelled them to turn back for Plymouth (from which the *Mayflower* later set out alone).

Kingswear, on the east side of the river, is the last stop on the **Torbay and Dartmouth Steam Railway** (reached from Dartmouth by passenger ferry). The railway starts in Paignton.

◆
DORCHESTER
Dorset

The county town of Dorset retains much of its atmosphere as coaching-stop and rural market. It features in both these guises in the novels of Thomas Hardy, who called it Casterbridge. Hardy was born in a cottage near by at **Higher Bockhampton** and lived at **Max Gate**, a house he built to his own design on the outskirts of town, for the last 43 years of his long life. **St Peter's Church**,

Grey's Bridge across the River Frome, the **King's Arms** and **White Hart** hotels all feature in his novels. The huge 2,000-year-old earthworks of **Maiden Castle** are two miles (3km) away.

◆◆
EXETER
Devon

Exeter is one of Britain's historic cathedral cities, its older parts grouped around the great Norman-into-Gothic structure and spilling downhill to the river, once the site of a substantial inland port. This is another town that has been tidying itself up to meet the latter years of the century. Inevitably, a visit begins with the **cathedral**. From outside it is extremely handsome, with flying buttresses and Norman twin towers tightly packed with decoration, including many blind arches. Most remarkable is the West front with 80 statues. Inside, the whole of the nave, or at least the upper part of it, is visible at once, with a vista sweeping past the screen and organ (1665) so that the eye can make the most of ribbing flowing upwards out of fluted columns to form elaborate fan vaulting.

The cathedral close is calm and lovely, with buildings of many periods all round, among them black-and-white **Mol's Coffee House** and the elegant flat front of the **Clarence Hotel**. In St Martin's Lane, just off the close, is the **Ship Inn**, supposedly beloved of Sir Francis Drake. In the High Street, also adjacent, is the oldest British **Guildhall** in use. All of this is more or less on top of the hill rising above the River Exe. Walking in almost any direction from here, one soon encounters the substantial remnants of the much-patched city walls, built on Roman foundations. Downhill to the Exe is the recently refurbished harbour area. Here, among the old warehouses, there are antique shops, pubs and tearooms, not to mention an excellent collection of boats in the **Maritime Museum**.

◆
EXMOOR
Devon and Somerset
This moor, which forms a National Park, was once hunting ground preserved as Royal Forest. Today it is mostly open country, rising to 1,700 feet (518m). Grazed by sheep, cattle and ponies, it is less dramatic than Dartmoor but can also be on the bleak side – though again it positively sparkles in fine weather. **Lynmouth**, **Porlock**, **Minehead** and **Dunster** are the main centres of population on or near the sea. The moor proper, setting for Richard Blackmore's romantic tale of *Lorna Doone*, lies inland.

◆◆
GLASTONBURY
Somerset
Glastonbury is one of the most spine-tingling sites in all of Britain, dense with layers of legend. You can see why the moment you set eyes on it, a little town at the foot of a steep tor, the whole set in flat green land that shines with surface

water all the winter. It is easy to imagine, as is in fact the case, that the tor and its small surrounding area of raised ground were once an island – reputedly the Isle of Avalon to which King Arthur set sail after the final battle against his nephew, Mordred. The strange markings on the surface of the hill are the remains of medieval agricultural workings. On the top stands a handsome tower, all that remains of the 14th-century church of **St Michael**. Below, near the middle of the town, a great **abbey** grew up. Here in 1191 the monks conducted an excavation, announcing they had found the bones of Arthur and Guinevere – royally reinterred in 1278 in the presence of King Edward I. Yet another legend asserts that Joseph of Arimathea, Christ's uncle, brought the holy baby here to Avalon, incidentally planting his staff in the ground. The resulting thorn-tree, generations of thorn-tree later, is reputed to flower on Christmas Eve. The legend is the origin of William Blake's famous poem which begins *'And did those feet in ancient time walk upon England's mountains green?'* Glastonbury Abbey fell into spectacular ruins with Henry VIII's Dissolution of the Monasteries. The abbot, Richard Whiting, was hanged, drawn and quartered on top of the tor. Now surrounded by acres of green grass, the abbey is a lovely place to wander through.

LAND'S END
Cornwall

Land's End has high, dramatic cliffs, with theatrical spikes and crags of rock rising from the sea. No better place, you might have thought, for contemplating the rigours of nature, especially when gales blow and great waves crash against the cliffs. In fact, the whole of Land's End has been tamed and turned into a kind of maritime and local Cornish theme park, with everything from a hotel and museum displays to a thunderous and thoroughly ambitious audio-visual show, featuring wrecks and wreckers – the front of a whole ship dashed upon the rocks – smugglers, lifeboatmen, even a hologram of the Arthurian magician, Merlin. Some hate it all; many love it.

LIZARD
Cornwall

This green but otherwise mostly bare peninsula protrudes to the south of Cornwall, to qualify as the southernmost point of England. It terminates with a lighthouse, one or two sad cafés and a small establishment making souvenirs and *objets d'art* in serpentine, a pretty brownish stone flecked in many colours. The landward side of the peninsula is given a ghostly touch by the huge post office satellite dishes of Goonhilly. Around the peninsula there are some beautifully precipitous small bays.

The edge of the world? Land's End

MARLBOROUGH
Wiltshire

Historically, Marlborough owes its importance to its strategic position on the London–Bath Road. The wide High Street is the most attractive feature of the town. It gives the impression of being a spacious, enclosed square, dominated at either end by two churches. The street is arcaded and most of the older buildings are from the 18th and 19th centuries: the town was gutted by a series of fires in the 17th century. An Act of Parliament that followed forbade the use of thatched roofs in the centre of town, hence the lovely mellow red brick houses with tiled roofs and tile-hung façades.

THE SOUTHWEST

◆
PENZANCE
Cornwall

Penzance, like Paignton and
Torquay, is sited on a south-
facing bay. It has a beach and
harbour, a few palm trees here
and there and it offers ferry
and helicopter services to the
Scilly Islands.

On the eastern approach to
Penzance, a short diversion
will bring you to the coast at
Marazion, a long straggle of
village around a point. Rising
from the sea is the conical
granite form of **St Michael's
Mount**, topped by a rather
domesticated castle. It is no
match for Mont St Michel in
Normandy, but it was for
centuries the centre of
Cornwall's tin exports. It is
reached by causeway at low
tide.

Newlyn lies just to the west of
Penzance, with a fishing
harbour and wholesale fish
market between itself and the
larger town. The village of
Mousehole, crushed in tight
around its fishing harbour, lies
a mile or two beyond. Cornish
is an ancient Celtic language
closely related to Welsh, and it
was here, in the 18th century,
that the last native Cornish-
speaker is said to have lived.

◆
PLYMOUTH
Devon

Plymouth was largely
destroyed by German
bombing during World War II
and for this reason is
sometimes considered of
limited interest to visitors. This
is a mistake. It is true that the
1940s and '50s city centre is a
little dull, but the history along
its waterfront, which survived
to a surprising degree, is
remarkable by any standard,
and Plymouth is an important
naval and garrison town.

On the **Hoe**, or 'High Place', a
protective ridge of stone rising
between the city centre and the
sea, stands **Smeaton's Tower**, an
early version of the Eddystone
Lighthouse in broad red and
white stripes, which has been
dismantled and re-erected on
dry land. It was on the Hoe, in
1588, that Sir Francis Drake was
playing bowls (an outdoor
bowling game) when news was
brought to him that the Spanish
Armada had been sighted; and
it was from Plymouth that the
English fleet sailed out to attack
the Armada, until, punished by
storm and cannon shot, it totally
disintegrated. Also on the Hoe
is the contemporary **Plymouth
Dome**, a cross between
museum and entertainment,
with diverting and informative
displays and a lively audio-
visual introduction to
Plymouth's history.

On the east side of the Hoe lies
the **Barbican**, with its old
fishing harbour, Jacobean and
Elizabethan houses, a gin
distillery (previously a
monastery), tourist shops and
the spot where the Pilgrim
Fathers descended to board
the *Mayflower*. A plaque
celebrates this voyage, as well
as pioneering journeys to other
distant parts, and the return of
the first trade unionists, the
Tolpuddle Martyrs, after their
exile in Australia.

On the far side of the Hoe,

where the River Tamar meets the sea to separate Plymouth (and Devon) from Cornwall on the further bank, the handsome early 19th-century naval buildings are still in military use. Across a further neck of land protecting the ferry port there lies a little staging post called **Admirals' Hard**. From here, a passenger ferry crosses the Tamar, providing access to **Mount Edgcumbe**, a country seat destroyed during the last war and now rebuilt as a centre of varied and romantic gardens on the headland guarding the river mouth.

A few miles inland towards the fringe of Dartmoor, Admiral Sir Richard Grenville converted the former **Buckland Abbey** into a handsome home. His house rises up inside the structure of the abbey tower.

◆◆
ST IVES
Cornwall
This pretty little resort on the northern side of the toe of Cornwall, with good beaches and harbour and plenty of retired residents, has long attracted painters, potters and sculptors. The chief reason for a pilgrimage is to visit the **museum** in the former studio of the sculptor Barbara Hepworth. Hidden away behind high walls right in the middle of town, it has a garden and workshops as well as the big studio-bedroom in which she died, in a house fire, in 1975. House and garden now offer a luminous celebration of her work.

◆◆
SALISBURY
Wiltshire
The diarist John Evelyn wrote in 1654 that Salisbury would be 'one of the sweetest Townes in Europe' if the buildings and streets were cleaned up and the streams cleared. Modern Salisbury cannot be faulted in these respects and is indeed a town of charm and substance. The town was moved to its present site from Old Sarum, two miles (3km) away, in 1220. Here it prospered, in a fertile convergence of the three rivers of Avon, Bourne and Nadder. The great **cathedral** was built and mostly completed in only 38 years –

Salisbury's Cathedral and lofty spire

hence its unified Early English style. Its spire was added later, the tallest in England. The view of the cathedral from the water meadows was a favourite of John Constable's. Memorable though the interior of the cathedral is, with magnificent chapter house, cloisters modelled on Westminster Abbey and the Library housing one of the four copies of the Magna Carta, it is its setting that makes most people catch their breath. It stands in the middle of wide green lawns, bordered by a walled close of gracious old buildings, **Mompesson House**, open to the public, and the **Bishops's Palace** among them. The old part of town is charming; many of the streets are preserved in their original medieval layout and the ancient market place is still in use. If you can negotiate the modern traffic conditions, Salisbury is an excellent base for touring Stonehenge and other sights on the Plain.

◆◆◆
STONEHENGE AND AVEBURY
Wiltshire

Stonehenge lies 8 miles (13km) north of Salisbury on the southern edge of the Salisbury Plain. Pictures of the stones and even the sight of them from a distance do not prepare you for their awesome size when you get closer. The stones, uprights with connecting lintels, were originally placed in the shape of two circles around an inner horseshoe, erected at various intervals between 3000BC and 1000BC. Some of them, weighing about 50-60 tons (50,800-60,960kg), were local, but others were brought from Wales. Their precise purpose has never been fathomed. The major axis of the stones was aligned with the position of the sun in midsummer and, even now, Stonehenge is a place of pilgrimage for many who attempt to hold Druidic

Mystery surrounds Stonehenge

services here at the summer solstice. Unfortunately, to limit access to these enthusiasts, the stones have been fenced off. The standing stones at **Avebury** are equally impressive, however, and are entirely accessible.

Of the original 700 or more stones, placed in three circles and enclosed by a ditch, many have disappeared. Nevertheless, the stone assembly remains extraordinarily powerful.

Silbury Hill, 5 miles (8km) west of Marlborough, is a great green artificial mound, 50 feet (15m) high with sheep grazing on the lower slopes. The hill is said to represent the labour of 700 men over a period of 10 years but its purpose remains a mystery. There is no direct access and the best view is from the parking lot below.

West Kennet Long Barrow is an early Stone Age burial site, west of Silbury Hill. The main chamber and passages are accessible.

Giant white figures cut into the chalky hillsides, many of them thousands of years old, are as mysterious a feature of the English landscape as the standing stones. The best known are the 180-foot (55m) **Cerne Abbas Giant** in Dorset, the **Long Man of Wilmington** in Sussex and the **White Horse** near Uffington, in Oxfordshire.

◆
TINTAGEL
Cornwall
Tintagel is an obligatory objective for those with an interest in King Arthur, Guinevere and the Knights of the Round Table. There is little to see except the romantic ruins of a **castle** perched on the rocky northern shore of Cornwall; nor is the little town a place of beauty. But the legends surrounding Tintagel are compelling. Arthur was supposedly born here, some hundreds of years before the construction of the present castle, and here he lived with Guinevere, presiding over his chivalrous knights.

◆◆
WELLS
Somerset
Wells deserves a visit from all who might enjoy a gently curving little High Street packed with coaching inns, a **bishop's palace** ringed by a tranquil moat, one of the loveliest cathedral closes in all England and a superlative **cathedral**. Water flows continuously in open gutters beside the High Street and has done so since it was diverted here in 1451. The cathedral is famous above all for the great mass of sculpture, 300 out of 400 statues surviving, scattered across its west end and nestling in niches even around the backs of its twin towers. Inside, it has an extraordinary feature, an arch above an arch, tapering at the bottom, installed later on to support the endangered central tower. There are many other notable features, ranging from a fine chapter house to the adjacent 'Vicars Close', a retreat composed of small stone houses.

The **Cheddar Gorge**, a limestone rent in the peaceful-looking Mendip Hills, begins 8 miles (13km) to the northwest. Impressive to the British, less so perhaps to visitors from countries on a larger scale, it is surprising because of its location in peaceful countryside. It offers opportunities for rock-climbers; caves are plentiful.

Accommodation
Bath

The Priory, Weston Road (tel; (0225) 331922) has been converted into a particularly comfortable hotel. Relaxing amenities and friendly service are provided at the **Lansdown Grove**, Lansdown Road (tel: (0225) 315891), a traditionally run hotel with magnificent views of the city. **Haringtons**, 9–10 Queen Street (tel: (0225) 461728) is a small, family-run hotel and restaurant which is set in a quiet, attractive cobbled street in the city centre.

Exeter

The White Hart, 65 South Street (tel: (0392) 79897) offers character, charm and cosiness. Guests can choose to eat in the wine bar, coffee shop or extensive *à la carte* restaurant. The family-owned **St Andrews Hotel** at 28 Alphington Road (tel: (0392) 76784) has light, comfortably furnished rooms and a cheerful dining room. Guests can choose between *à la carte*, hot buffet and bar snack menus at the **Red House**, 2 Whipton Village Road (tel: (0392) 56104) on the outskirts of the city.

Penzance

The Queen's Hotel, The Promenade (tel: (0736) 62371) is a large, traditional hotel on the seafront. Locally caught Newlyn fish is a speciality. **Higher Faugan Hotel**, in Newlyn (tel: (0736) 62076), offers individually furnished rooms and a short set menu.

St Ives

The **Garrack Hotel**, Higher Ayr (tel: (0736) 796199) has 21 rooms, an indoor swim-/spa-pool, sauna and solarium and a reputation for good food. The **Chy-an-Drea**, the Terrace (tel: (0736) 795076) offers a homey atmosphere.

Salisbury

The 13th-century **Red Lion Hotel**, Milford Street (tel: (0722) 23334), is famous for its courtyard, charm and antiques. The **White Hart**, in St John Street (tel: (0722) 27476) serves a varied cuisine, and the **County Hotel**, in Bridge Street (tel: (0722) 20229) offers comfortable, well-equipped rooms. Close to the shops and Cathedral Close, the **Cathedral Hotel**, Milford Street (tel: (0722) 20144) has a lively public bar.

Restaurants
Bath

Garlands, 7 Edgar Buildings, George Street (tel: (0225) 442283) is a small restaurant offering French modern style cuisine. **Popjoys**, next to the Theatre Royal in Beau Nash House, Sawclose (tel: (0225) 460494) offers imaginative and enjoyable dishes.

PEACE AND QUIET

Wildlife and Countryside in England
by Paul Sterry

The English countryside is renowned for its green and lush appearance. This is due, in part, to the mild climate. The country benefits from its proximity to the Atlantic Ocean and the Gulf Stream, usually ensuring both generous rainfall and freedom from prolonged temperature extremes in summer and winter.

In fact England offers the perfect case-history in which to trace the way the natural world has adapted to co-exist with man's interference. Although much of the landscape looks entirely natural, virtually all of it has been adapted in one way or another. Most open countryside is agricultural land and even woodlands are, or were until recently, managed in some way. Although this has not always been to the benefit of the country's natural history heritage, there are some habitats, notably chalk downland and coppiced woodland, whose rich diversity owes much to man's activities. Many of the most interesting places are contained within nature reserves. It was not until much of England's natural heritage had been destroyed or disfigured – largely in the years after World War II – that conservationists and the public realised just how much was being lost to agribusiness, housing, roads and development of all sorts. Despite the work of numerous

Cumbria's dramatic scenery

conservation bodies and public awareness of 'green issues' the destruction goes on. Official responsibility for nature conservation in England falls primarily on English Nature, a government body which attempts to safeguard threatened species, partly by legislation and partly through ownership and/or management of nature reserves. Each county has an independent naturalists' trust, which owns or manages nature reserves. Two of the largest conservation bodies, the Royal Society for the Protection of Birds (RSPB), and the National Trust are among the country's biggest landowners. There are numerous other privately owned nature reserves, and in recent years many local authorities have taken up the management of country parks, local nature reserves, etc.

PEACE AND QUIET

National Parks

England has eight national parks. They were established to maintain the appearance and heritage of the land within their boundaries, but, although conservation areas and nature reserves may be found within them, seemingly incompatible activities such as commercial forestry, intensive farming and even mining are also carried on. All the National Parks have excellent information centres which can provide information on wildlife, walking, accommodation and so on.

Dartmoor National Park

This is a large area of heather moorland and bogs, with impressive granite outcrops and wooded valleys adding to the variety. Despite the numbers of visitors, this is one of the few places in southern England where you can find really wild landscapes. The wildest parts of the moor lie north and west of Postbridge, on the B3212, but for a more accessible taste, walk from the parking lot at either Bellever (just southwest of Postbridge) or Fernworthy reservoir (northeast of Postbridge). Both these places have signposted trails. On the east side of the moor, try Haytor Down, on an unclassified road west of Bovey Tracey. Here you will find superb examples of the granite outcrops called tors which are such a feature of Dartmoor. A little to the east of Haytor is Yarner Wood, a nature reserve that protects some of the moor's finest surviving oakwoods. On the

moor's west side is Lydford Gorge, off the A386, which has superb waterfalls and is an excellent place to look for birds and wildflowers.

Exmoor National Park

Exmoor has heather moorland and wooded valleys somewhat similar to Dartmoor but with a wider variety of scenery – some more dramatic and some more pastoral. Horner Woods (south of Porlock) and the valley of the River Barle (between Dulverton and Withypool) are excellent places to explore a mixture of ancient valley woodlands and river scenery. For more open, moorland scenery, Webbers Post (south of Porlock) is an excellent place to begin. South again is Dunkery Beacon, the highest point of the moor and a superb viewpoint. This is as good a place as any to look for red deer. The coastal scenery at Woody Bay, Heddon's Mouth and Hartland Point is dramatic, as is the wooded Lyn Valley. Exmoor is famous for its ponies and for its red deer; the ponies are everywhere but the deer are shy, and patience is needed to seek them out.

Norfolk Broads National Park

The most recent National Park, only established in 1990, the Norfolk Broads is an area of reedbeds, open water channels, alder carr woodland and grazing marshes. Many areas have been adversely affected by pollution and changes in water chemistry, but Martham Broad (near Great Yarmouth) and Hickling Broad (near Stalham) remain excellent places for wildlife. Specialities among the insects include swallowtail butterfly and Norfolk aeshna dragonfly, while unusual plants include marsh sow-thistle and milk parsley. Marsh harriers, bearded tits and bitterns are three of the most exciting bird species that you are likely to see. Strumpshaw Fen (near Norwich) is a good place for wetland birds.

Peak District National Park

Considering its proximity to several large cities in middle England, it is not surprising that this park is extremely popular and sometimes crowded. Two main types of rock bring strong contrast here. Where the underlying rock is millstone grit ('the dark peak') the vegetation is acid loving and often dominated by heather moorland and bracken. On limestone ('the white peak') the flora is more varied, and Lathkill Dale National Nature Reserve is especially good. There are trails through beautiful scenery in Dove Dale and in the Manifold and Hamps Valleys. Also explore Monsal Dale, Taddington Dale and Chee Dale, all west of Bakewell. These are good areas for birds. One of England's rarest and most showy plants, Jacob's ladder, has its stronghold here. The nearby Ladybower Reservoir (near Sheffield) is good for birds of moorland and mature conifers.

Yorkshire Dales National Park

Much of the scenery in this park is quintessentially English

– lush, green meadows, well-maintained stone walls and beautiful stone buildings. Dramatic limestone scenery – rocky outcrops and weathered sidewalks – add to the variety. Malham Tarn (near Skipton) is especially worth visiting, both for the birds on its waters and for the birds and plants in its vicinity.

North York Moors National Park

This park includes large stretches of grouse moorland which are regularly burned on a rotational basis to encourage new growth in the heather, so that there are young, juicy shoots for the red grouse, which are consequently common here. (This is not a magnanimous gesture; the grouse are shot for sport and

Heather moors in North Yorkshire

the table.) On the coast, Robin
Hood's Bay provides a scenic
alternative with dramatic cliffs
and seascapes.

Northumberland National Park

Moorland and steep valleys,
many of which are wooded,
form the principal landscapes
here. The rivers are the haunt
of birds such as dippers and
grey wagtails; buzzards,
curlews, redstarts and ring
ouzels should all be seen
elsewhere. One of the best
ways to capture the feel of this
park is to follow the course of
the River Coquet upstream
from Rothburn to Chew Green,
on the wild Cheviot slopes.
Nearby sites include Budle
Bay (near Bamburgh) for
mudflats and shore birds, and
Holy Island and Lindisfarne
Nature Reserve for excellent
dune flowers and coastal
birds.

Lake District National Park

This famous region contains
England's most dramatic
mountain scenery. The
grandeur of the peaks –
Scafell Pike is the highest at
3,205 feet (977m) – is matched
by the splendour of the dozen
or so lakes. The Lake District
gets very crowded in summer,
so try to come either in spring
or autumn when it looks better
anyway. The colours of the
autumn vegetation – especially
birch and bracken – are
stunning. You stand a good
chance of seeing red squirrels
here; they are very patchily
distributed throughout the rest
of England. Golden eagles
attempt to breed here in their

only English site. Wast Water
has the highest mountain and
the deepest lake, side-by-side
– while Ullswater is wooded
and has wild daffodils.

The following places are
described from west to east
and south to north.

The Scilly Isles

These islands lie west of the
Cornish mainland and are
reached by helicopter or boat
from Penzance. They have a
wide variety of habitats, from
dramatic sea cliffs to sandy
beaches and sheltered fields
to reedbeds. Covered in
colourful flowers in spring, the
Scillies are a haven for migrant
birds (and birdwatchers!) in
the autumn. The main island, St
Mary's, is very varied. The
maritime heath and cliffs on
Penninis Head contrast with
the sheltered Porthloo beach,
frequented by large numbers
of waders during the winter.
The Holy Vale trail is good for
ferns, mosses and migrant

Prawle Point, South Devon

birds, while hides overlooking the lake at Porth Hellick are also worth a visit. Other islands can be visited by launch; Tresco is one of the most popular destinations. Famous for the Abbey Gardens, with an excellent collection of sub-tropical plants, it also has freshwater lakes and extensive patches of maritime heath. The little island of St Agnes is a birdwatcher's favourite. The tiny fields, sheltered by tall hedges, are regularly visited by rare migrant species in the autumn.

West Cornwall

The Cornish coast is undeniably spectacular. Battered by Atlantic gales, the cliffs here are covered in flowers in springtime and offer bracing walks throughout the year. The Land's End area is well known and very popular, but nearby Porthgwarra is equally dramatic and attracts fewer people. The Lizard peninsula is as famous for its unusual flowers as it is for its scenery. Outcrops of serpentine rock favour botanical rarities, while the more common but equally beautiful thrift and sea campion are widespread and colourful. Kynance Cove is especially attractive.

South Devon

South Devon has a wonderful coastline, much of it still unspoilt. The shoreline is rich in marine life and colourful flowers brighten the cliffs. Prawle Point, south of Kingsbridge, with its red soils and patchwork of small fields, is particularly inspiring. This is a good spot for migrant birds in spring and autumn and lucky observers may see a cirl bunting, a resident speciality of the area, and one of England's rarest birds. The male's striking black and yellow head markings make him unmistakable. Nearby Slapton Ley is also a favoured site for birdwatchers. This large freshwater lake is separated from the sea by a shingle beach which is excellent for bracing walks. The lake itself is fringed with reedbeds and marsh. It is the haunt of breeding warblers as well as thousands of migrants and winter visitors. Berry Head Country Park, east of Brixham, is a dramatic limestone headland with marvellous wild flowers. Dawlish Warren Nature Reserve and the Exe estuary in general are excellent for waders, wildfowl, gulls and sea ducks. The sand dune flora at Dawlish Warren is excellent and is at its best from June to August.

Cheddar Gorge

Although this deep, limestone gorge is besieged by tourists, it has considerable geological and wildlife interest. The wild flowers, in particular, are outstanding. To get away from the crowds try Ebbor Gorge, a few miles to the south. The flowers here are nearly as good and you might see a badger on one of the excellent nature trails at dusk.

Slimbridge Wildfowl Trust

Throughout the year, Slimbridge's outstanding wildfowl collection, maintained on man-made pools, is well worth visiting, although during July and August the male ducks are likely to be moulting and may look rather inelegant. During the winter months, the grazing marshes and pools attract thousands of wild birds, including large numbers of Bewick's swans.

Dorset resident: a chalkhill blue

The Forest of Dean

The forest lies in Gloucestershire, close to the border between England and Wales. It was once a Royal hunting forest but is now a rather loose mixture of plantation woodland, with areas of natural oak woodland on acid soils with beech and ash on lime-rich areas.
One of the best places to see the birds of the forest is at the Nagshead RSPB Reserve near Cinderford; Symond's Yat, near Monmouth, across the Welsh border in Gwent, is worth visiting not only for the spectacular views but also for views of nesting peregrine falcons and woodland flowers.

South Dorset

From Portland to Chesil, the Dorset coast has both scenic beauty and wildlife interest. The Isle of Portland, near Weymouth, is an important migration spot for birds. There is a small seabird colony here with puffins, guillemots and fulmars on the west cliffs, and the limestone flora is good in undisturbed areas. Chesil Beach, which connects Portland to the mainland, has a rich and fascinating flora, and the Fleet – the lagoon behind the beach – is good for shorebirds at low tide. Near by, Radipole Lake and Lodmoor Country Park (both in Weymouth) are excellent for waterbirds, and can also bring surprises; Radipole, for example, has Cetti's warblers. The stretch of coast between Lulworth and Swanage is dramatic and has exciting geological features. Seabirds breed on the cliffs at Durlston Country Park and the limestone-loving flora along the coastal path includes such specialities as sea cabbage and bee orchid. Insects, too, are varied and include chalkhill blue and Lulworth skipper butterflies, great-green bush-crickets and stripe-winged grasshoppers. Poole Harbour and Studland Heath National Nature Reserve are also good for shorebirds and heathland flora and fauna respectively.

The New Forest
Although parts of the New Forest are wooded – both with areas of native trees and with conifer plantations – much of the land is open heathland comprising gorse, ling, bell heather and cross-leaved heath. The forest as a whole is one of Europe's premier wildlife sites.

New Forest birds
Look out for these species:
Buzzard
Redstart
Hawfinch
Wood Warbler
Hobby
Nightjar
Dartford Warbler
Stonechat
Hen Harrier
Merlin
Short-eared Owl
Great Grey Shrike

Any suitable area is worth exploring, but the parking lots at Beaulieu Road Station, Hatchet Pond and Fritham are particularly convenient.

The Seven Sisters Country Park
Situated between Seaford and Eastbourne, this area combines dramatic chalk cliffs with excellent areas of chalk downland, a threatened habitat once typical of the Sussex South Downs. Among the chalk-loving flowers are several species of orchids. Insects include stripe-winged grasshoppers and chalkhill blue butterflies.
The shingle beach at the mouth of the River Cuckmere has an interesting flora, while behind it, a lagoon provides sanctuary for breeding and feeding birds. The channelled river has remnants of saltmarsh along its banks and the cut-off meanders are good for gulls, ducks and waders. Nearby Seaford Head Nature Reserve has migrant birds and a good chalk flora, and Friston Forest is a mature plantation woodland. The cliffs at Beachy Head can be walked to from the country park.
The whole area is noted for its migrant birds, both common and unusual, but for greater variety – although a far bleaker landscape – visit Dungeness near the Sussex/Kent boundary. The RSPB has a reserve here with hides overlooking flooded gravel pits.

Stodmarsh National Nature Reserve
Situated a few miles to the east of Canterbury in the Stour Valley, this is a large area of open water, woodland, reedbeds and marsh. The

reserve is viewed from a raised bank known as the Lampen Wall. The birdlife is rich and varied. Cetti's warblers, bearded tits and water-rails are year-round residents. Migration time brings thousands of swallows, martins and swifts. In winter, the wildfowl numbers build up and visitors may see several hen harriers in the air at once, quartering the reedbeds in search of prey.

Nearby sites include Church Wood RSPB Reserve, on the western outskirts of Canterbury, which is good for woodland birds.

Windsor Great Park and Virginia Water

An area of ancient parkland and open water, the park contains many venerable, gnarled oaks as well as more recent plantations. The older trees attract a variety of birds and insects, some of the latter being especially rare in Britain.

Virginia Water is full of wildfowl in winter. Naturalised mandarin ducks breed here and grey herons fish around the shores. Even if you miss every bird in the place, the colours of the trees in autumn make a trip worthwhile.

Both these areas have clear paths and offer hours of walking in beautiful surroundings.

Minsmere RSPB Reserve

This is the RSPB's showpiece reserve, and is open to the general public every day except Sundays. It is situated on the Suffolk coast between Southwold and Aldeburgh. Careful management maintains a mixture of reedbeds and open water, on which avocets – elegant black and white waders which are the symbol of the RSPB, and uncommon in England – nest. Even if you are not an avid birdwatcher Minsmere should give you some pleasure; it is a beautiful place, with signposted walks and a quarter of an hour spent in one of the many hides may just allow you to spot (with help!) a really unusual or rare bird.

The North Norfolk Coast

This stretch of coastline has a lot of surprises in store for visiting naturalists. Cley and Salthouse Marshes are a mecca for birdwatchers, having produced an extraordinary range of rarities over the years. View the marshes either from Cley Beach or from Cley East Bank. A permit can be bought for the Norfolk Naturalist's Trust reserve at Cley. Blakeney Harbour has extensive areas of mudflats and saltmarsh which are feeding grounds for waders, wildfowl and gulls. Blakeney Point, reached either by boat or by walking along the pebbly beach, has tern colonies and colourful dune flowers in summer. Common seals haul out on the sand banks and beach to sunbathe. Titchwell RSPB Reserve is another good spot to see breeding terns and waders and wildfowl. Further inland, small relics of Breckland grassland can be found between Thetford, Mildenhall and Lakenheath. Weeting Heath Norfolk Naturalists' Trust Reserve (permit required from warden) safeguards a small but significant area.

Bempton Cliffs RSPB Reserve

Bempton's dramatic chalk cliffs are situated near Bridlington, on the east coast. Pride of place here goes to the nesting gannets – Britain's only mainland colony of these birds – but puffins, guillemots, kittiwakes and fulmars add to the interest. Most species can be seen sooner or later at eye level as they ride the updraughts off the cliff face. The cliffs are sheer and very dangerous so be careful and do not stray from the prescribed areas.

The Farne Islands

Without a doubt, the Farne Islands offer one of England's great wildlife spectacles. The islands, reached by boat from Seahouses, on the windswept northeast coast, are owned by the National Trust and were effectively the first British nature reserve; St Cuthbert, who lived here 1,300 years ago, decreed that the eider ducks in particular should be completely protected. Today's visitors have to keep to prescribed paths, with the result that the nesting birds have lost most of their fear of man. On Staple Island, shags build untidy nests of seaweed and flotsam within a few feet of the path, and guillemots, kittiwakes and puffins can be seen at close range. On Inner Farne, Arctic terns are

A puffin outside its burrow

numerous and dive-bomb human intruders, sometimes drawing blood with their attacks (take a hat with you and wear it all the time!). Despite their aggression, birds will often settle within a few feet of quiet observers. Eider ducks are also unbelievably confiding.

Leighton Moss RSPB Reserve

Situated at Silverdale, near Carnforth, in Lancashire, this reserve comprises a mixture of reedbeds, fens and alder carr woodland. An area of saltmarsh adds to the variety. For access to the reserve and to the hides, a permit must be bought at the reserve centre. Highlights include bitterns and otters, both of which are regularly seen here, but are very difficult to find elsewhere in England.

Near by, Arnside Knott has fine limestone scenery with associated wild flowers. Be sure to keep to the footpath to avoid damaging this valuable habitat.

FOOD AND DRINK

In recent years there has been something of a renaissance in the English kitchen. New generations of cooks, self-taught and owing no allegiance to the grand classical traditions of European cuisine, have opened their own restaurants and won the recognition of international judges. New British Cooking has not yet filtered through into the general consciousness. But for the discerning visitor who did not expect to eat well in England, there is a surprise in store. Despite calorie and cholesterol counting, the English breakfast lives on: fruit juice, cereal or porridge, eggs (fried, scrambled, boiled or poached), bacon, sausage, mushrooms and tomatoes, not to mention regional variations like smoked haddock, kippers and black pudding (blood sausage). All this with toast, tea or coffee.

Lunch in a pub is generally a convivial occasion. You can stand at a bar, exchanging news and views with the locals, or sit by the fire, or, in the summer, eat your meal at a garden table outside. Most pubs offer a choice of hot and cold food. Lasagne and chili con carne are often on the same menu as the traditional ploughman's lunch (thick slices of cheddar cheese on french bread with pickles and salad) and other British staples such as steak and kidney pie, but beware: in some pubs the food can be microwaved and pretty tasteless.

There are endless opportunities to eat Italian, French and Spanish food. Even cheaper are other 'ethnic' cuisines like Chinese, Indian, Malaysian and Thai. Japanese restaurants, though, are never cheap. In London and the larger cities, the choice is further extended by US-style fast food, African, Caribbean and Middle Eastern food. Sunday lunch is one meal which, for many people, is still traditionally English: roast beef or lamb and Yorkshire pudding, roast potatoes, gravy and vegetables, with a sweet dessert to follow.

As for drink, there is tea; then there is beer. It may taste warm and flat to those used to the icy exuberance of lager, but it is worth persevering if you are in search of the real England. Different regions have local breweries all producing a subtly different brew. It is a rather different story with wine: there are vineyards scattered round the country but their output is small and undistinguished.

SHOPPING

The English have been called a nation of shopkeepers, and that is good news for the visitor. Every town has a multiplicity of chain store and retail outlets as well as a host of speciality shops. The chief of the chain stores is **Marks and Spencer**, known for the quality of its goods and competitive pricing. **Boots the Chemist** and **W H Smith** the newsagents also appear in most High Streets.

London remains the mecca of consumerism for choice and quality, but other provincial cities like Bath and Chester are highly rated. The Bull Ring in Birmingham is one of England's biggest shopping centres. In London, **Burberry's** and **Aquascutum** in Regent Street sell the sort of casual but elegant clothes that are traditionally English. Still in Regent Street, no self-respecting parent could possibly leave the capital without buying a gift to take home from **Hamleys**, the huge toy store on five floors. High fashion British designers like **Jasper Conran** and **Bruce Oldfield** have shops a safe distance away at Beauchamp Place in Knightsbridge. England is awash with **antiques**. In London, street markets like **Portobello Road** and **Bermondsey** often have an entertainingly eclectic assortment. Major auction houses like **Christie's** and **Sotheby's** process an enormous amount of goods – furniture, paintings and jewellery – through their salerooms. The smartest – that is, the most expensive – showrooms of antique furniture are to be found in New Bond Street: step into **Partridges** or **Mallett and Son**.

In Brighton, on the south coast, the Lanes are full of antique shops. Bath is littered with them. Towns in the south like Midhurst, Petworth and Dorking are good for browsers and buyers alike.

For **books**, London's **Foyles**, in Charing Cross Road, is probably the best known, but the vast number of volumes and the small number of assistants can make shopping here a confusing experience. There are other specialist bookshops on the same road. The university bookshops like **Dillons** in London and Oxford, **Blackwells** in Oxford and **Heffers** in Cambridge have a wide selection. The **Travel Bookshop** in Notting Hill was the first of its kind and is still the best known in London. **Hay-on-Wye**, at the foot of the Black Mountains on the Welsh border, is a whole town entirely devoted to books – second-hand and antique books as well as prints.

For **souvenirs** of England that will not weigh your suitcase down, look in the gift shop attached to the stately home, castle or museum that you are visiting. For instance, the shop at the **British Museum** sells reproductions of the early Minoan jewellery it displays in its cabinets; at **Shakespeare's House** in Stratford-upon-Avon you can buy English soaps and pot-pourri and varieties of tea. Street markets are still a lively feature of smaller cities and towns.

If you spend a lot of money shopping, it might be worth getting back the VAT on the goods you are taking home with you. Fill in a form from the shop, get it stamped at customs before you leave, send the form back to the shop and they will refund the tax. But you will have to carry the goods in your hand luggage to be inspected by customs.

ACCOMMODATION

Take your pick from a suite in
a grand country house to
camping in a field. And there
is everything in between,
including hotels, motels, youth
hostels and self-catering
accommodation.
The most popular choice for
those touring the country is
Bed and Breakfast, or B&B.
You get a bed for the night in a
private house and breakfast
before you leave the next
morning, and many now have
en suite bathrooms or showers.
At their best, they offer the
generous hospitality of
ordinary people in their own
homes; at their worst, they are
indifferent overnight
accommodation supervised by
a landlord. Tourist Information
Centres will reserve you a
B&B in advance (there may be
a small fee). You could also
contact the **World Wide Bed
and Breakfast Association**
(tel: (071) 370 7099).
The **country house hotel** is like
a rather grand B&B (and lunch
and dinner) in a rather grand
house. Here, the guests may
be treated as members of a
house party, invited to help
themselves to drinks, read in
the library and join the family
for dinner. But leave your
children at home: many
country house hotels do not
allow guests under a certain
age. Between the sublime and
the ridiculous, there are
ordinary hotels in all
categories. Large hotel chains
like **Trust House Forte**
(tel: (081) 567 3444) are reliable
in terms of quality and are

found in central locations. There
are also roadside hotels and
lodges on major motorways and
trunk roads – such as the
Granada chain (tel: (05255) 5555).
Several private agencies offer
self-catering options: ask at the
local Tourist Information Centre.

CULTURE, ENTERTAINMENT AND NIGHTLIFE

London is the cultural nerve
centre of the country. Its
theatres, concert halls and
galleries are famous worldwide.
While there is a symphony
concert at the Royal Festival
Hall, an opera at Covent Garden
and an exhibition at the
Hayward Gallery, there is also
jazz at Ronnie Scott's Club in
Soho, a poetry reading in an
East End pub and an
experimental play at the King's
Head pub in Islington. Stratford
has a vigorous theatrical life
(see page 60) and there is
plenty going on in the other
major English cities.
In Birmingham, there is the
City of Birmingham Symphony

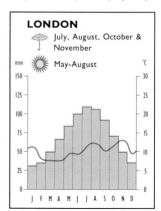

Orchestra and the Repertory Theatre, the first in the country and still going strong. Manchester has its Royal Exchange Theatre and the City Art Gallery with a fine collection of pre-Raphaelite paintings. Provincial theatre, art and music are often some of the best in the country, despite the concentration of funds in the capital.

As for entertainment and nightlife, nightclubs abound in every city. There are listings in local papers.

WEATHER AND WHEN TO GO

England enjoys a temperate but unpredictable climate. Summers are not usually very hot but can be humid. Winters are rarely very cold but they can be bone-chillingly damp. Late spring and early autumn are just about perfect – but still unpredictable. The western half of the country is more prone to rain but it is only a question of degree – it can and often does rain everywhere. Pack an umbrella and do not step out without sufficient layers of clothing to shed or add as required.

HOW TO BE A LOCAL

The most successful way to be a local is to remind yourself of all the common stereotypes of the English (the stiff upper lip, the reserve, the respect for order) then do your best to forget them. Yes, Londoners travelling in a crowded train do stare down at their newspapers and do not address each other, but if you should ask one of them for directions, you will undoubtedly meet with a friendly response. And in other parts of the country you will find locals far more forthcoming and chatty.

Pubs play an important part in English social life. They are a place to meet friends before an evening out, to unwind at the end of a day's work, play a game of snooker (a variety of billiards) or darts and

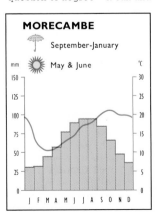

MORECAMBE

September-January

mm May & June ℃

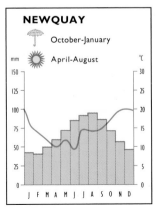

NEWQUAY

October-January

mm April-August ℃

to catch up on the gossip. Wine bars are a newer phenomenon. They have the reputation of being fashionable and more expensive, but provide less opportunity to strike up a conversation.

The tradition of the fish 'n' chip shop or 'chippy' lives on – the home-grown English fast food take-out. The only new developments are that the chippy is also likely to be a Chinese take-out and the fish and chips are not wrapped in newspaper. But one thing remains constant: you have to take your place in the line.

It is more fun and, in many ways, easier, to be a local away from the cities. Watch a weekend cricket match sitting in a deck chair on the edge of a village green; eat a bag of vinegary mussels from a stall at the seaside and walk on the beach with your trousers rolled up to your knees, or stand at the pub bar and discuss Saturday's big (soccer) match. The best way to be a local is to talk about the weather. Smile and offer a greeting. 'Good morning. Lovely day, isn't it?' will break down any English reserve.

CHILDREN

There is a huge variety of supervised children's activity for periods ranging from one day to a fortnight. They can learn to sail, climb, windsurf, act, play a musical instrument, take photographs or learn about computers. **PGL Young Adventure Holidays**, Alton Court, Penyard Lane, Ross-on-Wye, Hereford HR9

5NR (tel: (0989) 764211) is just one of the many companies catering to children.

Museums are no longer stuffy, dull places where children peer into glass cases and learn things. The **Jorvik Museum** in York, the **Beamish Open Air Museum** near Durham and the **Tullie House Museum** in Carlisle are supreme examples of how the new interactive and 'hands on' approach makes a trip to the museum something to nag your parents for. The **Museum of the Moving Image**, an encyclopaedic, multi-media experience of film on London's South Bank, often has a long line of children impatient to get in. Bradford's **National Museum of Photography, Film and Television** has the same draw. There is also **Madame Tussaud's** in Marylebone Road, and the South Kensington museums in London . . . the list is endless. Theme parks are entertainment centres for the whole family. **Alton Towers** near Stoke-on-Trent is one of the best. Its biggest rival is **Thorpe Park**, near Chertsey in Surrey. Rides with names like the Flying Fish roller coaster and the Family Tea Cup offer a stomach-churning clue to what you might expect.

The modern environmentally-aware child is not as enthusiastic about zoos as its parents. For a sight of wild animals roaming free visit the **Wild Animal Kingdom** in the grounds of Woburn Abbey in Bedfordshire or **Marwell Zoo** near Winchester.

TIGHT BUDGET

- Bed and breakfast accommodation is usually cheap, cheery and a good way of meeting local people.
- Bus travel is slower but certainly cheaper than rail travel. For discount travel you can buy tickets such as the Tourist Trail Pass for bus travel from major bus stations.
  There are various rail discount tickets such as Britexpress; ask at major railway stations.
- Eating ethnic (Chinese, Indian, Thai, Greek) is excellent value in England. Fish and chips are filling and basically nutritious.
- Eat a hearty English breakfast if that is included in the price of your room. It might last you through much of the day.
- If you are travelling with children, package tour operators can usually negotiate better hotel bargains than you can independently. Children sharing your room may pay half price or nothing at all, depending on their age.
- July and August are the most expensive months to travel in England. It is also a time when places of interest are crowded and the roads busy with traffic.

SPECIAL EVENTS

February: Jorvik Viking Festival, York.
May: Chelsea Flower Show, at Royal Hospital, London. Well-dressing, Tissington,

Fun with the dolphins on land!

Derbyshire (Ascension Day). Corpus Christi Carpet of Flowers and Floral Festival, Arundel Cathedral, London Road, Arundel, West Sussex. Cheese-rolling Ceremony , Cooper's Hill, near Gloucester. Bath International Festival of Music and the Arts.
May-August: Glyndebourne Festival Opera Season, Glyndebourne, near Lewes, East Sussex.
June: Trooping the Colour, Saturday nearest 11 June, Horseguards' Parade, Whitehall, London. Scarborough Fair, Scarborough (third week), North Yorkshire.
June-August: Royal Academy of Art Summer Exhibition, Royal Academy of Arts, Piccadilly, London.
July: Cheltenham International Festival of Music, Cheltenham, Gloucestershire.
August: Three Choirs Festival, alternately in Worcester, Gloucester and Hereford.

September: Blackpool Illuminations, Blackpool, Lancashire.

November: Guy Fawkes Day: bonfires and fireworks on 5 November to commemorate Fawkes' failure to blow up Parliament in 1605.

Lord Mayor's Procession and Show, The City, London. There are countless other carnivals, arts, drama and music festivals around the country: ask at the Tourist Information Centre for details.

SPORTS

Cricket

A very English sport which has been called 'chess on grass'. It is transformed into something more resembling 'dominoes on grass' in the more aggressive playing style of the Australians or West Indians. The main cricket venues in London are Lord's Cricket Ground in St John's Wood and The Oval in Kennington. Outside London try Headingly (Leeds), Old Trafford (Manchester), Edgbaston (Birmingham) and Trent Bridge (Nottingham) where the test (international) matches are played. The season lasts from April to the end of September.

Horseracing

The flat racing season runs from March to early November and the most famous meetings (attended by members of the royal family) are the Epsom Derby in Surrey and Royal Ascot in Berkshire. Other major meetings are held at Newmarket in Suffolk, Goodwood in Sussex and Doncaster in Yorkshire. The Grand National Meeting, the most famous steeplechase, takes place at Aintree racecourse in Merseyside. Show jumping enthusiasts go to Wembley in London for the Royal International Horse Show (July) and Horse of the Year Show (October).

Rowing

The Oxford and Cambridge University Boat Race takes place on the Thames between Putney and Mortlake in March each year. Henley hosts Royal Regatta each July.

Rugby

Rugby Union is the amateur branch of the game played by professionals as Rugby League. Rugby Union Centre is at Twickenham, near London, and the big event is the Five Nations Tournament between England, Scotland, Ireland, Wales and France.

Soccer

Soccer, or football, as it is more commonly called in England, is the most popular national game. Matches take place each Saturday and on some Sundays throughout the season (gradually extended from August to May), culminating in the FA (Football Association) Cup Final held at Wembley Stadium at the end of May.

Tennis

The Wimbledon Lawn Tennis championship takes place in June-July at the curiously named All England Lawn Tennis and Croquet Club, in Wimbledon, London.

DIRECTORY

Contents

Arriving
Camping
Crime
Disabled People
Driving
Electricity
Embassies and
 Consulates
Emergency
 Telephone
 Numbers

Entertainment
 Information
Health Regulations
Holidays
Lost Property
Media
Money Matters
Opening Times
Personal Safety
Pharmacies
Places of Worship

Post Offices
Public Transport
Senior Citizens
Student and Youth
 Travel
Telephones
Time
Tipping
Toilets
Tourist Offices

Arriving
Entry formalities

Nationals of the US and Canada, Western European countries outside the EC, Australia, New Zealand, Japan and South Africa need a valid passport and must complete a landing card as they enter. European Community member citizens need a valid passport/national identity card. Nationals of other countries must have a visa. You may bring into the country without paying duty 200 cigarettes, 1 litre of spirits, 2 litres of wine and 60cc/mls of perfume if you are 18 years and older.

Airports

Most travellers arrive in England through Heathrow airport (tel: (081) 759 4321/745 7432), at the western reaches of London, or through Gatwick (tel: (0293) 31299/28822), in Sussex. Both airports have excellent and frequent connections with the capital and between each other. Taxis are expensive. From Heathrow, it is a journey of 45 minutes by bus or underground train into London's city centre. From Gatwick, a 30-minute train ride takes you to London's Victoria station. Frequent buses connect Heathrow and Gatwick. Other major airports include Birmingham (tel: (021) 767 5511) and Manchester (tel: (061) 489 3000).

Banging the drum for May Day

DIRECTORY

Camping

The uncertain weather, even in the summer when camping sites are open, make this a risky choice for a vacation. However, the British AA's guide to **Camping and Caravanning in Britain** lists a wide selection of sites; and the **Camping and Caravanning Club**, Greenfields House, Westwood Way, Coventry CV4 8JH (tel: (0205) 694995) produces its own magazine.

Crime

Ostentatious displays of wealth are likely to attract the wrong kind of attention but, in general, crime against tourists is not a major problem. Take the usual precautions. Keep cars locked and hold on to your money in a crowd.

Disabled People

Provisions for disabled people are improving in England but standards vary throughout the country. The wheelchair symbol denotes special facilities, but it is vital to check with hoteliers, etc, direct.
RADAR (the Royal Association for Disability and Rehabilitation) at 25 Mortimer Street, London W1N 8AB (tel: (071) 637 5400), provides information and advice.
William Forrester is a guide, himself disabled, who organises tours (tel: (0483) 575401).

Driving

You need a current driving licence or an International Driving Permit to drive in England. All the main international car rental companies have offices in major cities. Most will insist you have held your driving licence for at least one year, and some that you are at least 21 years old before they rent you a car. *The Highway Code*, published by Her Majesty's Stationery Office (HMSO), is the official rule book of the road, available at booksellers and stationers.

Drive on the left, pass on the right. Give priority at junctions and rotaries to those approaching from the right. The driver and front seat passenger must wear a safety belt. If back seat passengers are children, they must wear seat belts, when available. Pedestrians have priority on zebra crossings (black and white lines across the road). Motorways are designated by the letter M before the road number. There are no tolls to pay, except on the Severn and Humber Bridges. Main roads carry the letter A and minor roads are B roads. Speed limits on motorways are 70mph (112kph), 30mph (48kph) in built-up areas and 60mph (96kph) on most other roads.

Gas is not cheap, but is among the cheapest in Europe. Both unleaded and ordinary 4-star gas is widely available.

In the event of a breakdown on a motorway, pull over to the hard shoulder, put on hazard lights and place a warning triangle behind the car. Get everyone out of the car by the passenger doors. Use the emergency telephone by the side of the motorway to call for assistance and then stay with your car until help arrives.

Electricity
220-240 volts, 50 cycles. Most hotels have dual plugs for electric razors. US appliances will require an adaptor.

Embassies and Consulates
United States Embassy: 24 Grosvenor Square, London W1A 1AE (tel: (071) 499 9000). **Australia High Commission**: Australia House, Strand, London WC2B 4LA (tel: (071) 379 4334). **Canada High Commission**: 38 Grosvenor Street, London W1X OAB (tel: (071) 629 9492). **New Zealand High Commission**: New Zealand House, Haymarket, London SW1Y 4TQ (tel: (071) 930 8422).

Emergency Telephone Numbers
Dial 999 anywhere in the country. The operator will connect you with fire, police or ambulance services.

Entertainment Information
All Tourist Information Centres and hotels are good sources of local entertainment information. Most national newspapers have listings of events in London and the major provincial cities. Local newspapers are also good sources of information.

Health Regulations
No vaccinations are required to enter the United Kingdom. Any animal must remain in quarantine for six months to comply with British anti-rabies regulations.
If you have a serious accident or need emergency medical

care, you will be treated free of charge on the National Health Service. Otherwise you are charged as a private patient. Citizens of countries in Western Europe and the European Community, Australia, New Zealand and Hong Kong, which operate a reciprocal arrangement with Britain, are mostly exempt from payment but should check the details. All other nationals should be adequately insured before they travel.

Holidays
1 January; March/April: Good Friday, Easter Monday (variable); First Monday in May, last Monday in May, last Monday in August are all Bank Holidays; 25 and 26 December.

Lost Property
Report serious losses – passport, credit cards etc – to the police. For lost passports, inform your embassy, who will be able to issue emergency documents. Loss of credit cards must be reported immediately to issuing company.
For property lost on the buses or subways of London, write or go to **London Transport Lost Property Office**, 200 Baker Street, London NW1 5RZ.

Media
Media are diverse, reflecting a broad range of opinion. Among daily newspapers, there are popular tabloids like the *Sun* and the *Daily Mirror*, newspapers with a conservative tendency like *The Times* and the *Daily Telegraph*, and those with a liberal tendency like the *Guardian* and *Independent*.

On radio the BBC broadcasts on five national channels ranging from modern pop to classical music and serious documentary and education programmes. The BBC World Service can also be heard here. The BBC also runs local radio stations, and there is a network of commercial (independent) radio.

Of the four national television channels, BBC1 and BBC2 are financed by central government and viewers' licence fees. Channel 4 and ITV are independent and financed by the advertisements they carry. Satellite and cable television is available to subscribers.

Money Matters

The pound sterling (£) is worth 100 pence or p. Coin denominations are 1p, 2p, 5p, 10p, 20p, 50p, £1, £2. Notes come in £5, £10, £20, £50. Get the best rate of exchange at a branch of one of the main banks – Barclays, Midland, Lloyds or National Westminster. Bank opening hours are 9:30A.M.–3:30P.M., Monday–Friday. Some branches are open on Saturday mornings. Credit cards are widely accepted.

Opening Times

Offices are open Monday–Friday from 9:00A.M.–5:30P.M.. Shops are open from 9:00A.M.–5:30 or 6:00P.M. Monday–Saturday. Shops in smaller towns may shut for an hour in the middle of the day and one afternoon a week. In the larger towns, there is at least one late night shopping, and supermarkets now tend to be open later. You can often find small grocers in towns which open very long hours. Museums and art galleries are open from 9:00 or 10:00A.M.– 5:00 or 6:00P.M. (Sundays from 2:00P.M.). Winter opening hours can be restricted. Open-air sites close at dusk (around 4:00P.M. in the winter) and many country houses are shut altogether out of season. Many sites are run by councils, companies and individuals and their opening times may vary.

Personal Safety

As a stranger in an unfamiliar environment, it makes sense to keep to well-lit and well-frequented areas, particularly if you are alone.

Pharmacies

There is usually one pharmacist in every town which is open beyond ordinary shop hours – the name and address is usually posted on any pharmacy door. The local police also have lists of pharmacists on duty after hours.

Places of Worship

Although the Church of England is the established church in England, every major (and minor) Christian denomination has a place of worship. There are also synagogues, mosques and temples. Addresses can be found in local Yellow Pages. Further information from: the **Church of England Enquiries Centre** (tel: (071) 222 9011); the **Catholic Central Library** (tel: (071) 834 6128); the **Islamic Cultural Centre** (tel: (071) 724 3363) or the **Board of Deputies of British Jews** (tel: (071) 387 4044).

Post Offices
Open Monday-Friday, 9:00A.M.–5:00P.M. (most open at 9:30A.M. one morning a week) and on Saturday 9:00A.M.–1:00P.M.. Sub-post offices close 1:00–2:00P.M. on weekdays and on Saturdays at either noon or 12:30P.M..

Public Transportation
On most public transportation, children under five travel free. Those between five and 15 and senior citizens (men over 65 and women over 60) travel at a reduced rate.
Trains are the fastest method of travelling any distance in England. Frequent inter-city services connect all major cities at a speed of 125 mph (200km). There are standard and first class carriages. You are advised to reserve a seat when travelling in the rush hour. There are various travelcards, cheap day roundtrips and rail rover tickets which save money. The BritRail Pass (available from outside the country from the overseas offices of British Rail or their agents) is a good value for those touring the whole of Great Britain by train. They offer unlimited rail travel for four, eight, 15, 22 days and a month. Victoria Coach Station is the main London terminal for long distance express buses, which are slower but cheaper than rail travel; information from **National Express**

A roof boss in Southwark Cathedral

Coaches, (tel: (071) 730 0202). Taxis are usually available at main railway stations; in London you can hail them in the street. London has a subway network (the 'tube'), as does Newcastle, and Liverpool's underground line carries passengers from main line to local stations.

Senior Citizens
Some concessions on public transportation are available to senior citizens. British Rail, for instance, offers reduced rate fares on production of a senior citizens' Railcard. To find out more enquire at the local Town Hall or Tourist Information Centre (and carry proof of your eligibility).

Student and Youth Travel
Young people between the age of five and 15 travel on all public transportation at reduced

rates. An identity card showing date of birth is a useful accessory. London Regional Transport requires children of 15 to carry a 'photocard' as proof of age. For 16 to 25-year-olds, the BritRail Youth Pass offers reduced rate unlimited rail travel. The ticket must be purchased abroad and is valid for use throughout the United Kingdom. A student bus card (available from Victoria Coach Station, London SW1 and National Express agents) will reduce the price of bus travel by a third. You must be 17 and over and a full time student. The National Student Discount Card (bought before you arrive) offers reductions on a host of things, including car rental. Details from **NSDC**, PO Box 190, London WC1.

Telephones
Some phone booths are operated by cash and require money to be inserted before dialling. Others are operated by phone card (purchased from post offices and newsagents). Insert the card and the cost of your call is automatically debited from it. There are phone booths which only work with a credit card.

Useful Numbers
192 for directory enquiries.
100 for the operator.
155 for the overseas operator.
To make an international call, dial 010 followed by the country code and area code minus the initial 0. Country codes are as follows:
United States and Canada:1
Australia: 61
New Zealand: 64

To call Britain from abroad, tel: 44.

Time
England is on Greenwich Mean Time (GMT) in the winter, five hours ahead of US EST. In the summer (last Sunday in March to last Sunday in October) the clocks go forward one hour ahead of GMT.

Tipping
A service charge of 12–15 per cent is usually included in most hotel and some restaurant bills. You should tip waiters, porters, maids, taxi drivers and hairdressers. Do not tip in a cinema, theatre or a pub.

Toilets
Follow signs to a 'Public Convenience' or 'WC' if not designated by a symbol. You sometimes need a 2p or 10p piece to operate the door.

Tourist Offices
British Tourist Authority, Thames Tower, Black's Road, London W6 9EL (written enquiries only).
All large towns and cities have Tourist Information Centres. A full list is given in the English Tourist Board's free booklet *Tourist Information Centres in Britain*.
BTA offices abroad
USA: 40 West 57th Street, New York, NY 10019 (tel: (010 1) 212 5814700).
Australia and New Zealand: Associated Midland House, 171 Clarence Street, Sydney, NSW 200 (tel: (010) 61 2 29 8627).
Canada: Suite 600, 94 Cumberland Street, Toronto, Ontario M5R 3N3 (tel: (010 1) 416 961 8124/925 6326).

INDEX

Page numbers in italics
refer to illustrations

accommodation (see
    also individual
    regions) 116, 119
airports and air
    services 121
Aldeburgh 39
architectural styles
    11–14, 15
Arundel 82–3
Audley End 47, 47
Avebury 103

Bath 94–5, 95
Battle 83
Beaulieu 87
Belgravia 34
Berwick-upon-Tweed
    68, 68
Blenheim Palace 50–1
Boston 40
Brighton 83
Bristol 92
British Museum 30, 30
Brixton 34
The Broads 40, 106–7
Brontë Parsonage
    Museum 69
Buckingham Palace and
    the Mall 24, 24–5
budget tips 119
Bury St Edmunds 40
Buxton 59

Cambridge 13, 41,
    41–2
camping 122
Canterbury 84, 84–5
car rental 122
Carlisle 69
Chatsworth 59
Cheddar Gorge 104,
    110
Chelsea 34
Chester 51–2
Chichester 85–6
children's
    entertainment 118
Chinatown 23
Chipping Campden 53
climate and seasons
    117

Colchester 42
Cotswolds 52–3, 53
Covent Garden 23
Coventry 53–4
crime 122

Dartmoor 96, 96, 106
Dartmouth 97
Dedham Vale 42–3
Design Museum 33
disabled travellers 122
Docklands 31
Dorchester 97
Dover 86
driving 122
Dulwich 34
Durham 70, 70

Ely 43, 43
embassies and
    consulates 123
emergencies 123
English gardens 5,
    14–15
entertainment 116–17,
    123
entry formalities 121
Exeter 97–8
Exmoor 98, 106

Farne Islands 113
festivals and events
    119–20
Fleet Street 20
food and drink 114
Fountains Abbey 67,
    67

Glastonbury 98
Globe Theatre site 33
Gloucester 54
Grasmere 74
Greenwich 31–2
Guildhall 20–1

Hadrian's Wall 71, 71
Hampstead 34
Hampton Court 32, 32
Haworth 69
health matters 123
Helmsley 76
Hereford 49, 55
Highgate 34–5
history of England
    6–11

Holy Island 72, 72
Houses of Parliament
    25, 25
Hyde Park 29, 29

Imperial War Museum
    33
Ironbridge 55, 55–6
Isle of Wight 86

Kensington Palace 29
Kew Gardens 32
King's Lynn 43–4

Lacock Abbey 95
Lake District 72–5,
    108
Land's End 99, 99
Lavenham 44
legal district (London)
    21
Lincoln 45, 45
Liverpool 66
Lizard 99, 109
local etiquette 117–18
local time 126
London 16–35
    accommodation 35
    history 17, 20
    map 18–19
    sightseeing 20–35
lost property 123
Lowestoft 45–6
Ludlow 56

Madame Tussaud's
    30–1
Manchester 66
maps
    central England
        50–1
    Cotswolds 52
    East Anglia 38
    England 36–7
    Europe 6
    Lake District 73
    London 18–19
    north of England
        64–5
    Peak District 59
    south of England
        80–1
    south-west England
        92–3
Marlborough 99

INDEX/ACKNOWLEDGEMENTS

media 123–4
money 124
Monument 21
Museum of London 21
Museum of Mankind
 28

National Gallery 25
national parks and
 reserves 106–13
National Portrait
 Gallery 26
Natural History
 Museum 29
New Forest 87, 111
Newmarket 46
North York Moors *76*,
 76–7, 107–8, *107*
Norwich 46
Notting Hill 35, *35*

opening times 124
Oxford 56–7, *57*
Oxford Street 23

Peak District *58*,
 58–9, 107
Penzance 100
personal safety 122,
 124
pharmacies 124
Piccadilly Circus 23
places of worship 124
Plymouth 100–1
post offices 125
public holidays 123

public transportation
 125

Regent Street 23–4
Regent's Canal 31
Regent's Park 31
Richmond 77
Royal Academy 28
Rye 83

Saffron Walden 47
St Ives 101
St Martin-in-the-Fields
 26, *26*
St Paul's Cathedral
 21, *21*
Salisbury *101*, 101–2
Sandringham House 44
Scarborough 78
Science Museum 30
Scilly Isles 108–9
shopping 114–15
Shrewsbury 59
Sissinghurst Castle 88
Soho 24
South Bank Arts
 Centre 33
Southwark Cathedral
 33, *125*
sports and leisure 120
Stoke-on-Trent 60
Stonehenge 102, *102*
Stratford-upon-Avon
 60–1, *61*
student and youth
 travel 125–6

Sudbury 47

Tate Gallery 26
telephones 126
Thames Flood Barrier
 32
Tintagel 103
tipping 126
toilets 126
tourist offices 126
Tower Bridge 22
Tower of London 22,
 22
Trafalgar Square 26
Tunbridge Wells *87*,
 87–8

Victoria and Albert
 Museum 30
voltage 123

Warwick 61–2
Wells 103
Westminster Abbey
 26–7, *27*
Whitby 77–8
Whitehall 27
wildlife and
 countryside 105–13
Winchester 88–9
Windsor Castle 89,
 89, 112
Worcester 62, *62–3*

York 78–80, *79*
Yorkshire Dales 69–70

The Automobile Association wishes to thank the following photographers and libraries for their assistance in the preparation of this book.

NATURE PHOTOGRAPHERS LTD 105 Langdale Pikes (G A Lycett), 108/9 Prawle Point (A J Cleave), 110 Chalkhill blue (A Wharton), 113 Puffin (A J Cleave).

THE MANSELL COLLECTION LTD 17 Fire of London.

ANDY WILLIAMS Cover Ledbury.

ZEFA PICTURE LIBRARY (UK) LTD 35 Notting Hill Carnival.

All remaining pictures are held in the Association's own library (© AA PHOTO LIBRARY).